KS3 HISTORY
Third Edition

Industry, Invention and Empire

Britain 1745–1901

Aaron Wilkes

OXFORD
UNIVERSITY PRESS

Contents

Contents 2

Introducing KS3 History 4

A journey through time from 1745 to 1901 6

Chapter 1:
From farming to factories

1.1A What was Britain like 250 years ago? 8

1.1B What was Britain like 250 years ago? 10

1.2 Why did the population 'explode'? 12

1.3A No more homework! 14

1.3B No more homework! 16

1.4A How did factories create towns? 18

1.4B How did factories create towns? 20

1.5A Peter the pauper 22

1.5B Peter the pauper 24

1.6 What was 'black gold'? 26

1.7 A new 'Age of Iron' 28

1.8 The end of the 'Cripple Factory' 30

Chapter 2:
How was transport improved?

2.1 Turnpike fever! 32

2.2 Canal mania! 34

2.3 What were 'iron horses'? 36

2.4 Train reaction! 38

Chapter 3:
An age of invention

3.1A The National Awards for Invention and Design 40

3.1B The National Awards for Invention and Design 42

3.1C The National Awards for Invention and Design 44

3.2 What a good idea! 46

3.3 How great was the Great Exhibition? 48

3.4 So what was the Industrial Revolution? 50

Assessing Your Learning 1 52

Chapter 4:
Terrible towns

4.1A What made Sheffield stink? 54

4.1B What made Sheffield stink? 56

4.2 Welcome to Sickness Street 58

4.3A Who were the heroes of public health? 60

4.3B Who were the heroes of public health? 62

4.3C Who were the heroes of public health? 64

4.4 A class act? 66

4.5 Crimewatch 68

4.6 Catching the vile villains 70

4.7 Off to prison 72

4.8A HISTORY MYSTERY:

What did Jack the Ripper look like? 74

4.8B HISTORY MYSTERY:

What did Jack the Ripper look like? 76

Chapter 5:
The slave trade

5.1A What was the slave trade? 78

5.1B What was the slave trade? 80

5.2 What was it like on a slave ship? 82

5.3 A slave sale 84

5.4 A life of slavery 86

5.5A Why was slavery abolished? 88

5.5B Why was slavery abolished? 90

Chapter 6:
Britain vs. France

6.1A Britain versus France… in North America 92

6.1B Britain versus France… in North America 94

6.2A In what way is the execution of a
French king linked to Britain? 96

6.2B In what way is the execution of a
French king linked to Britain? 98

6.3 'Little Boney will get you!' 100

6.4A How did 'Nelson's touch' win the
     Battle of Trafalgar?   102

6.4B How did 'Nelson's touch' win the
     Battle of Trafalgar?   104

6.5 On board HMS *Victory*   106

6.6A Waterloo – Napoleon's last stand   108

6.6B Waterloo – Napoleon's last stand   110

Chapter 7:
The British in India

7.1 How did Britain get an empire?   112

7.2 What was India like before the British arrived?   114

7.3 Invasion of India   116

7.4A Indian mutiny… or war of independence?   118

7.4B Indian mutiny… or war of independence?   120

7.5 'The jewel in the crown'   122

Assessing Your Learning 2   124

Chapter 8:
The fight for rights

8.1A 1848: How close was a British revolution?   126

8.1B 1848: How close was a British revolution?   128

8.1C 1848: How close was a British revolution?   130

8.2 The match girls   132

8.3 Enough of history… what about *her*story?   134

Chapter 9:
A changing nation

9.1A Who cares?   136

9.1B Who cares?   138

9.2A What were Victorian schools like?   140

9.2B What were Victorian schools like?   142

9.3A A healthier nation?   144

9.3B A healthier nation?   146

9.4A George and the chocolate factory   148

9.4B George and the chocolate factory   150

9.5A What shall we do today?   152

9.5B What shall we do today?   154

9.6 The birth of modern football   156

9.7 The high street   158

9.8 Why is there a chimpanzee on a £2 coin?   160

9.9A The Great Hunger   162

9.9B The Great Hunger   164

Chapter 10:
What was Britain like by 1901?

10.1 How did Britain change between
     1745 and 1901?   166

Assessing Your Learning 3   168

Glossary   170

Index   173

Acknowledgements   176

Introducing KS3 History

Thinking about History

Before exploring this book, take a few minutes to think about these questions.

- What do you think history is?

- What have you learned in History lessons before? Did you enjoy the lessons or not? Think about why.

- Have you read any books about things that happened a long time ago? Have you watched any television programmes, films or plays about past events? Which ones?

So what is history?

History is about what happened in the past. It's about people in the past, what they did and why they did it, what they thought, and what they felt. To enjoy history you need to have a good imagination. You need to be able to imagine what life was like long ago, or what it may have been like to be involved in past events.

What about my History lessons?

Your lessons are designed to show you how, why and when things have changed through time. During the period in this book (1745–1901), Britain went through some of the biggest changes a country has ever known. From 1700 to 1800 the population of Britain more than doubled. And then, in the next 50 years, it nearly doubled again! The places where people lived changed dramatically too. Millions moved from the countryside to work in towns… which just grew and grew. In 1750, Oldham in Lancashire had around 300 inhabitants – but in 1821 it had 38,000!

The populations of Birmingham, Liverpool and Manchester all doubled too.

And things were changing abroad as well. The British began to make a big impact on a global scale, conquering countries, taking over land and fighting in wars and battles on land and at sea.

So you must be wondering how these things changed, and why they changed, and when. This book will take you on that journey of discovery… and hopefully turn you into a top historian on the way!

How does this book fit in?

This book will get you thinking. You will be asked to look at different pieces of evidence and to try to work things out for yourself. Sometimes, two pieces of evidence about the same event won't agree with each other. You might be asked to think of reasons why that is. Your answers might not be the same as your friend's or even your teacher's answers. The important thing is to give **reasons** for your thoughts and ideas.

How to use this book

Features of the *Student Book*, are explained here and on the opposite page.

Key to icons

Source bank · Film · Worksheet · History skills activity · Literacy · Numeracy

Depth Study

In each book, there is a mini depth study that focuses on a significant event or concept. These sections give you the chance to extend and deepen your understanding of key moments in history.

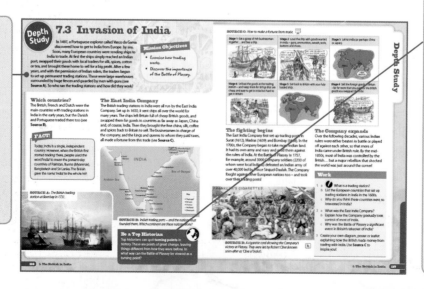

History skills

Be a Top Historian

Some tasks, ideas and sources will challenge you to think and act like a top historian and stretch your skills and abilities.

What Happened When?

This gives you an idea of what else was going on in the world at the same period you are studying in the lesson. It could also focus on a specific topic and make links across time, showing how things are connected.

Mission Objectives

All lessons in this book start by setting you 'Mission Objectives'. These are your key aims that set out your learning targets for the work ahead. At the end of each lesson you should review these objectives and assess how well you've done.

Wise Up Words

Wise Up Words are the really important key words and terms that are vital to help you understand the topics. You can spot them easily because they are in **bold red** type. Look up their meanings in a dictionary or use the glossary at the back of the book. The glossary is a list of these words and their meanings.

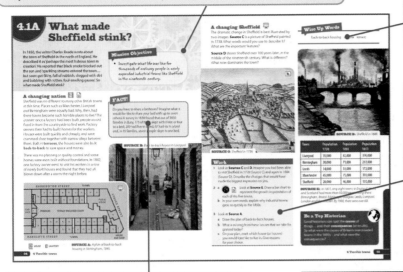

Work

Work sections are your opportunity to demonstrate your knowledge and understanding. You might be asked to:

* put events in chronological order
* explain how and why things changed over time
* work out why two people have different views about the same event
* discover what triggered an event to take place.

Fact!

These are the funny, fascinating and amazing little bits of history that you don't usually get to hear about! But in this series, we think they're just as important – they give you insights into topics that you'll easily remember.

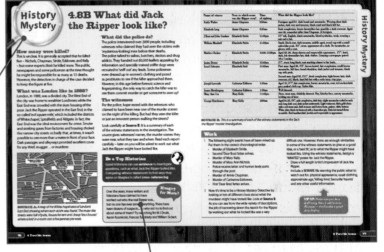

History Mystery

These sections give you an opportunity to pull all your skills together and investigate a controversial, challenging or intriguing aspect of the period, such as what 'Jack the Ripper' might have looked like.

Hungry for More?

You might be asked to extend your knowledge and research beyond the classroom. This is a time to take responsibility for your own learning. You might be asked to research something in the library or on the Internet, work on a presentation, or design and make something. Can you meet the challenge?

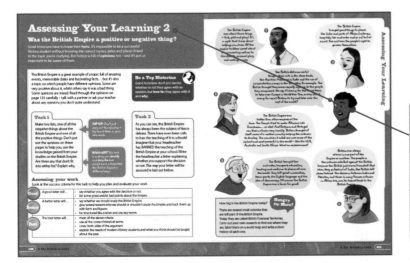

Assessing Your Learning

In the book, there are three extended assessments. These are opportunities for you to showcase what you have learned about the topic and to put your research and analysis skills to the test. Some are more creative, while some will focus on extended writing or looking at sources.

A journey through time from 1745 to 1901

This book covers the years from 1745 to 1901: the age of the Georgians and one of the most famous eras in British history – the Victorian period!

Some of the world's most famous people lived during this time and some of history's most remembered events took place then. It was a time of great change in Britain's towns and cities too – and in medicine, transport, invention, design, discovery and politics.

The timeline on these pages highlights some of these big events, significant people, new ideas, changes and discoveries. Read it carefully and then complete the work section.

1769

First cotton factory built by Richard Arkwright

1770

Captain Cook lands in Australia and claims it for Britain

1821

Electric motors are invented by Michael Faraday

1825

First public railway carries passengers between Stockton and Darlington

1832

Reform Act gives the vote to more men in Britain

1833

Slavery ends in the British Empire

1885

Motor car invented by Karl Benz

1876

Telephone invented by Alexander Graham Bell

1901

Queen Victoria dies

1879

Light bulb invented

1870

Elementary Education Act gives school places to all children

1865

Antiseptics invented

1783

United States officially becomes independent from Britain

1789

French Revolution leads to the execution of French king and queen

1796

Edward Jenner first uses vaccination against small pox

1801

Official union of Britain with Ireland

1805

Battle of Trafalgar: the British Navy defeats French and Spanish navies, giving Britain control of the seas

1812

Tin can invented

1803–15

Napoleonic Wars between France and other nations led by Britain; the French were defeated

1837

Victoria becomes queen

1845–52

Potato Famine begins in Ireland; about 1 million people die

1859

Charles Darwin publishes *On the Origin of Species,* which proposes the idea of evolution

Work

1 a How do you think the Victorian period got its name?
 b In the future, what do you think might be a suitable name for the period we are living in today? Explain your choice.
2 a Look at some of the inventions on the timeline. Pick out a few that you think made the greatest impact or changes. Give your reasons.
 b In the future, what modern inventions and discoveries (from the past 50 years, perhaps), do you think people will remember?

What was Britain like 250 years ago?

This book is about the people and the events of Britain between 1745 and 1901 – a time of great change. In fact, Britain probably changed more between these dates than during any other period in history. It was a time when the population grew faster than ever before and, by the end of the period, for the first time in Britain's history, more of the population lived in towns than in the countryside. It was a time when some of Britain's most famous battles took place – and when Britain gained an empire that rivalled any the world had ever seen. The period saw some of Britain's greatest inventors, politicians, medical men (and women), writers and businessmen come to the fore. And the foundations of many of our favourite sports, high street shops and familiar customs were also laid during this period. However, before we begin to investigate how much Britain had changed by 1901, we need to establish what Britain was like in 1745... so look through the following pages carefully.

Mission Objective

- Investigate what Britain was like in the mid-eighteenth century.

⚠ STOP AND THINK
Church records were not always accurate. Can you think of any reasons why they might not be? Clue: A costly registration. What problems does this cause historians?

So how many people were there?

About ten million people lived in Britain in the mid-1700s. However, it's hard to know the exact number because no one ever counted! Instead, historians have estimated the amount by analysing sources like church records. These list the number of baptisms and burials in any one church.

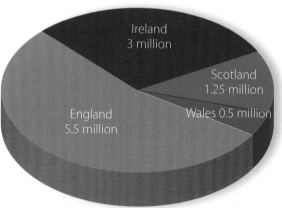

Ireland
3 million

Scotland
1.25 million

England
5.5 million

Wales 0.5 million

◀ **SOURCE A:** *A pie chart showing the estimated population in 1745. England's population was 5.5 million, Wales' 0.5 million, Scotland's 1.25 million and Ireland's population about 3 million.*

SOURCE B: *A painting of George III, king from 1760 to 1820. He was the best-known German ruler and was king for much of the early period covered in this book.*

◀ **SOURCE C:** *In the early 1700s the writer Daniel Defoe (who wrote* Robinson Crusoe *and the very rude* Moll Flanders*) published a travel book called* A Tour Through the Whole Island of Great Britain. *In this best-seller, he identified seven classes of people that he found on his journey.*

Different classes found on travels:

Class 1:	'The great who live profusely' [with lots and lots of money]
Class 2:	'The rich who live plentifully' [with lots of money]
Class 3:	'The middle sort, who live well'
Class 4:	'The workers, who labour hard but feel no want'
Class 5:	'The country people who manage indifferently [neither good nor bad]'
Class 6:	'The poor, whose lives are hard'
Class 7:	'The miserable, who really suffer'

Who ruled?

After Queen Anne (the last of the Stuarts) died in 1714, her distant German relative, George I from Hanover, came over to rule the country. In fact, there were at least 50 other members of the royal family who had stronger claims to be the next king or queen after Anne… but they were all Catholic! Instead, German-speaking Protestant, George, took the job. The new king, mainly due to the fact that he spoke no English, left Parliament alone to rule the country – which they loved! When George I died in 1727, his son (another George) took over.

By 1745 George II was king – but he wasn't particularly popular because it was said that he preferred Germany. Parliament continued to make laws and hold elections every few years. The king still had to agree with all their proposals before they became law… but Parliament controlled most of the king's money, so they never had much trouble getting his support! Rich men who owned lots of land were the politicians and only other rich men could vote for them. In fact, in 1750 only 5 per cent of men (the rich of course) could vote… and women couldn't vote at all.

FACT!

From 1760 to 1820, George III was king. He was the grandson of George II. People called him 'Farmer George'. Sadly, he suffered from periods of madness, during which time he ended every sentence with the word 'peacock'.

SOURCE D: *Downing Street was built in the 1730s and used as a home by some of the more important politicians. In 1735, George II gave house 'Number Ten' on Downing Street to Sir Robert Walpole, one of the politicians with whom he had been working closely. Other politicians teased Walpole for being so close to the king and called him '**prime minister**' as an insult ('prime' means first, number one or favourite). The nickname stuck and Walpole remained prime minister for years to come. Ten Downing Street is still home to Britain's prime minister today.*

How did people have fun?

The very rich read books in the vast libraries in their country houses, took walks in their landscaped gardens, boated on their lakes or got lost in their mazes. They went hunting, fishing, to concerts, to the ballet, and played billiards and dice. Poorer people went to the local pub, where they played skittles, bowls, cards and, of course, drank beer. During holiday times they went to fairs and gambled on bear-baiting and boxing.

SOURCE E: *A painting of a village fair, around 1710.*

How did people die?

People didn't know that germs caused disease. Basic operations, like removing an infected toenail, could result in death because there were no painkillers or germ-free operating rooms.

The big, killer diseases were smallpox (highly infectious, causing fever, blisters, scabs… and then death) and respiratory diseases, for example, pneumonia, bronchitis, diphtheria and tuberculosis, which affected breathing and the lungs.

The average age of death in Britain in 1745 was between 30 and 40 years of age, but some people lived long and healthy lives. Daniel Defoe (see **Source C**), for example, lived to 71 years of age. For every 1000 babies born, over 150 would die before they reached their first birthday… and one in five of the mothers would die too!

How did people get around?

Slowly – very slowly. There were no aeroplanes, trains or cars. Most people rarely left their village, except to go to the local town on market day. The roads were so bad that it could take up to two weeks to travel from London to Edinburgh… and four days to get from London to Exeter (and it's less than 200 miles away!). Some roads had been improved, but in 1745, they were a rare sight.

'We set out at six in the morning and didn't get out of the carriages (except when we overturned or got stuck in the mud) for 14 hours. We had nothing to eat and passed through some of the worst roads I ever saw in my life.'

▲ **SOURCE A:** *Adapted from the journals of Queen Anne in 1704. They were travelling from Windsor (in Berkshire) to Petworth (in Sussex), a distance of about 40 miles.*

SOURCE B: *Major industries and towns in the 1750s.*

Key
- Towns over 20,000 population
- Iron
- Coal
- Wool and cloth
- Cotton and silk
- Metal mining
- Agriculture

FACT!

Some of the world's best-quality fine china was produced by Josiah Wedgwood, based in Stoke-on-Trent. His goods were sold all over the world.

FACT!

Milkmaids sold milk around the city streets in open-top buckets. One customer wrote in his diary that on its journey around the city, the milk collected 'spit, snot, dirt, rubbish, sick and lice'. Enjoy your drink!

How did people make money?

Eight out of ten people lived and worked in the countryside ... and the vast majority were poor! They grew food and reared cattle and sheep. They grew enough to feed themselves and perhaps some extra to sell in the local town. Goods were made in people's homes or in small workshops attached to their homes. Some of the larger workshops in towns produced high-quality goods that were sold abroad. But even these businesses employed no more than 50 people. Everything a village or town needed was made by hand or on very simple machines – buttons, needles, woollen or cotton cloth, glass, bricks, pottery, candles and bread.

Some towns were growing fast (Liverpool, Leeds, Birmingham and Glasgow more than doubled in size between 1745 and 1800). Shopkeepers, chimney sweeps, flower sellers, doctors, housemaids, builders, cobblers and street traders all made a living in these fast-growing towns.

How 'Great' was Britain?

By 1745 Britain was becoming a major world power.

- The British controlled areas of land in many other countries. Parts of Canada, the West Indies, Africa, India and America were under British control.

- Britain imported Indian silk, jewels, pottery, ivory, tea, American coffee, sugar, tobacco and Canadian cod. Companies sold these around Britain or they were exported to other customers abroad.

- The goods made in Britain, like cloth, pottery and iron, were sold abroad in huge numbers. All this trade made a lot of money for British companies and provided plenty of jobs for British workers.

How 'arty' was Britain?

The eighteenth century was a great age for the arts. Daniel Defoe wrote *Robinson Crusoe*, Jonathan Swift wrote *Gulliver's Travels* and Samuel Johnson spent eight years writing the first ever *Dictionary of the English Language*. There were many great artists such as George Stubbs, Thomas Gainsborough and Joshua Reynolds, as well as world-renowned composers, such as George Frederick Handel, who came to live in England, from Germany, in 1710.

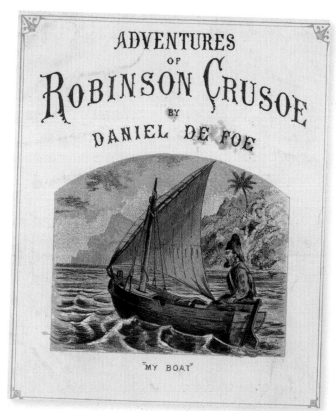

SOURCE C: *Daniel Defoe's* Robinson Crusoe *is still a well-known story today.*

Work

1 a Write a sentence or two about the origin of the term 'prime minister'.
   b In 1745, who was more powerful – the king or Parliament?
   c Write a sentence or two about your prime minister today. Before writing your answer, you may wish to discuss the role of your prime minister and their powers.

2 It is 1745. Pretend you are a foreign visitor, sent on a trip to Britain by a foreign king. You must prepare a fact file on Britain for your king back home. Use the following headings to help you:

- The people – How many? Where do they live? What do they do?
- The people in charge – Who runs the country? How? What about the royal family?
- Health of the nation – What were the common illnesses and diseases? How long could an average man expect to live?
- Travel – How advanced was Britain's transport system?
- 'Great' Britain – Were the British conquering other lands? If so, where and why?
- Leisure time – How did people have fun? How did this differ between rich and poor people?
- Culture – Who were the famous names in the fields of music, literature and painting?

Present your report as a TOP SECRET document – you never know what a foreign king might need the information for!

Why did the population 'explode'?

Between 1745 and 1901, the population of Britain grew so fast that one historian called it 'an explosion of people'. There were about seven million people living in Britain in 1745, with another three million in Ireland. By 1901, Britain's population was nearly 40 million. In other words, the population had more than quadrupled! So what was behind this 'explosion'?

There are only three possible ways for a population to increase:

i) the number of births can increase
ii) the number of deaths can decrease
iii) **immigrants** can move to the country.

Historians know that after 1745 the number of people moving to Britain was similar to the number of people leaving – so **immigration** couldn't have caused the population explosion. This leaves two other explanations!

Your task is to look through the following facts. Each has been identified by a historian as a cause of the population explosion between 1745 and 1901. Try to think whether the information in each fact would:

i) increase the number of births
ii) decrease the number of deaths
iii) do both.

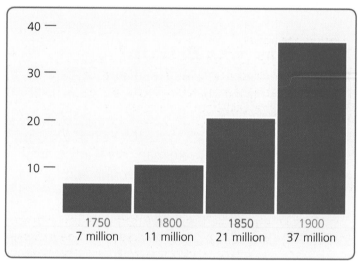

SOURCE A: *This graph estimates the population of Britain between 1745 and 1901. Following 1801, and every ten years after, a **census** was taken in England, Wales and Scotland. However, it didn't include Ireland's population.*

Fab farmers

After 1745, farmers produced more food. People had the opportunity to enjoy a healthier diet – fresh vegetables, fruit, meat, potatoes and dairy products. All the protein and vitamins helped the body to fight disease.

Magic midwives

After 1745, there were improvements in the care of pregnant women by **midwives**. Some hospitals were even providing **maternity** beds by 1760.

Smelly pants

From 1800, cotton started to replace wool as Britain's most popular cloth. Cotton underwear became very popular. Cotton is much easier to wash than wool, so regular washing killed off germs.

Young love

After 1745, people started to get married younger. This gave couples more time to have more children.

Jenner's jabs

In 1796, Edward Jenner discovered how to vaccinate against one of Britain's worst diseases – smallpox. Gradually, more and more people were treated until in 1853 vaccination was made compulsory for all. Eventually, smallpox disappeared.

Factory fever!

Arkwright's method of manufacture (and the huge profits he was making) inspired others to invent machines that produced cloth even more quickly and cheaply. In 1779, Samuel Crompton invented the **spinning mule**, which produced thread of a higher quality than Arkwright's. In 1785, Edmund Cartwright designed the **power loom**, which sped up the weaving process to the point where workers could keep up with the spinners. More and more factories were built and, by 1820, many people had left their villages and gone to work in factories. The domestic system was dying out – and being replaced by the **factory system**. As the factories grew, their owners built more and more houses for their workers to live in – and this was to lead to an even greater change to life in Britain.

'We used to gather potatoes before we came here. When not doing that, I used to mend fences or make baskets. We came to the factory five years ago, it's regular work you see. I work on spinning machines and my family still works with me. The wife helps a machine operator and the kids clean. Paid once a fortnight, family wage, in my pocket. Mind you, I miss the freedom. When you're your own boss, you work when you like. Now it's all clock, clock, clock...'

SOURCE A: *A factory worker in 1800.*

'Within the space of ten years, from being a poor man worth £5, Richard Arkwright has purchased an estate of £20,000; while thousands of women, when they can get work, must work a long day to card, spin and reel 5040 yards of cotton, and for this they have just four-pence or five-pence and no more.'

▲ **SOURCE B:** *An extract from An Impartial Representation of the Case of the Poor Cotton Spinners in Lancashire, 1780.*

'Wanted at Cromford. Frame-work-knitters and weavers with large families. Likewise children of all ages may have constant employment. Boys and young men may have trades taught them, which will enable them to maintain a family in a short time.'

▲ **SOURCE C:** *An advert from The Derby Mercury, 20 September, 1781.*

SOURCE D: *Cromford Mill in Derbyshire, one of the most important buildings in British, and world, history.*

Wise Up Words

factory system   power loom
spinning frame   spinning mule

Work

1 Explain what 'factory system' means.

2 a Match these descriptions to the numbers on the factory diagram.

- This waterwheel is turned by the river and provides power for the spinning frames in the factory.
- This clock lets the workers know exactly what time it is. Anybody late for work will be severely punished.
- The factory owner, who pockets all of the profits!
- These machines are running 24 hours a day, producing cloth.
- Men, women and children work shifts to operate the machines and receive a regular wage.

b Explain how Arkwright made higher profits despite selling his cloth for less money.

3 Look at **Source A**.
a In what ways has the factory system changed this worker's life?
b What do you think the worker means by 'clock, clock, clock…'?

4 Look at **Source B**. Does this source criticize or praise Richard Arkwright? Explain your answer carefully.

5 Read **Source C**. What do you think attracted people to Cromford?

6 **The Big Write!**

People came from all over the world to visit Cromford. Imagine you are a German visitor, who has to write a report for someone considering opening a factory. Describe how the factory operates, what you have seen and so on. Perhaps include a picture or diagram. In order to focus your writing, you must write no more than 150 words.

How did factories create towns?

Eight out of ten people lived in the countryside in 1745. The few towns that did exist were very small and their biggest buildings would have been a church or cathedral. But the new factories changed all this. So how did factories create towns? How were these factories powered if they weren't next to rivers? And what did these new towns look like?

Mission Objectives

- Explain how factories caused the population of towns to increase.
- Suggest reasons why steam engines replaced waterwheels as the source of power for factories.
- Evaluate the positive and negative effects that this new power source had.
- Analyse the significance of both Watt and Boulton.

The countryside empties

The new factories were like magnets. They pulled people from the countryside with the promise of regular work and good wages. When factory owners started to build houses for their workers, shops, churches and inns soon followed. Places that were previously tiny villages grew into large towns and small towns became huge, overcrowded cities. **Source A** illustrates how the building of a factory could lead to the creation of a large town. **Source B** shows how some of Britain's most famous towns and cities grew between 1745 and 1851. **Source C** shows where some of these major industrial towns were situated whilst **Source D** illustrates how one town – Bradford – grew in size from 1800 to 1873.

Population increases in some British towns			
	1745	1801	1851
Liverpool	35,000	82,000	376,000
Manchester	45,000	75,000	303,000
Leeds	14,000	53,000	172,000
Bradford	7,000	25,000	105,000
Birmingham	30,000	71,000	233,000

SOURCE B: *Factories towns saw huge population increase.*

Be a Top Historian

Top historians need to apply the skills they learn in other subjects, such as Geography, to help them. On pages 18–21 you can draw on what you've learned about the growth of settlements and population change in your Geography lessons.

▼ **SOURCE A:** *The birth of a town.*

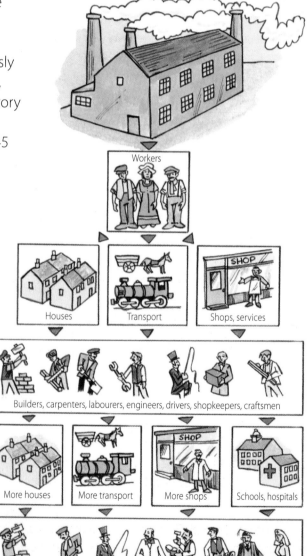

Workers

Houses | Transport | Shops, services

Builders, carpenters, labourers, engineers, drivers, shopkeepers, craftsmen

More houses | More transport | More shops | Schools, hospitals

More builders, labourers, drivers, shopkeepers, cobblers, tailors, teachers, nurses etc.

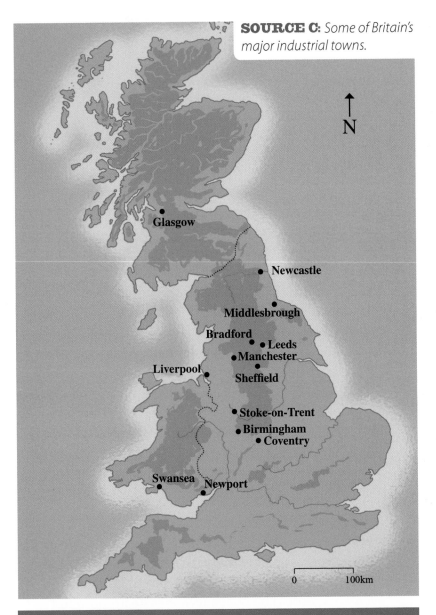

SOURCE C: *Some of Britain's major industrial towns.*

N

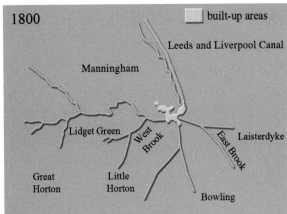

1800

built-up areas

Leeds and Liverpool Canal

Manningham

Lidget Green

West Brook

East Brook

Laisterdyke

Great Horton

Little Horton

Bowling

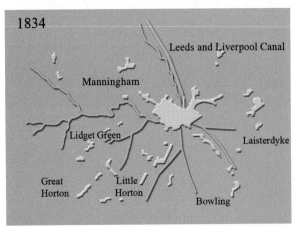

1834

Leeds and Liverpool Canal

Manningham

Lidget Green

Laisterdyke

Great Horton

Little Horton

Bowling

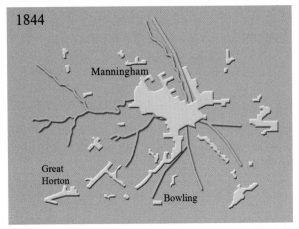

1844

Manningham

Great Horton

Bowling

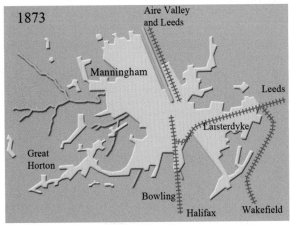

1873

Aire Valley and Leeds

Manningham

Leeds

Laisterdyke

Great Horton

Bowling

Halifax

Wakefield

SOURCE D: *A map which shows how Bradford expanded between 1800 and 1873.*

Work

1. Look at **Source A**. Imagine you have built a factory that is going to create a town. You must:
   - give your company a name
   - decide what product you are going to make
   - explain how you're going to attract workers
   - explain all the 'knock-on' effects their arrival is going to have.

   Finally, when you have explained how a town has been created, give your town a name.

2. **a** Turn the figures for one of the towns in **Source B** into a bar chart.

   b What does this source tell us about the growth of towns?

3. Look at **Source D**. In your own words, explain how Bradford expanded between 1800 and 1873. Use **Source D** and some of the information in **Source B** in your explanation.

I've got the power!

By 1800, factories were producing all sorts of things – and making their owners lots of money. But factory owners faced a problem. They wanted their machines to run 24 hours a day, 365 days a year in order to maximize their profits. Most of the early factories used water power – created by a huge wheel that would be turned by a river – to drive the machinery. But despite being free and clean, this water power had its problems (see **Source A**).

16 December: The river is frozen. Our waterwheel will not turn and we have no power. The workers have been sent home because their looms do not function.

29 May: The hot weather has made the River Ribble very low. In the afternoons, our looms go very slow.

28 August: Work has stopped in 30 mills in Blackburn. Work will not start until it rains again.

SOURCE A: *Based on a factory owner's diary, 1805.*

Full steam ahead!

Water power was just not reliable enough – so factory owners turned to a new form of power that scientists had been developing – the **steam engine**! These had first been used to pump water out of underground mines but they were slow, expensive and kept breaking down. Then, in 1768, a Scottish inventor named James Watt met a businessman called Matthew Boulton at a science club called the **Lunar Society** in Birmingham. Together they developed a new kind of steam engine that Watt had been working on. It included a new (**'sun-and-planet'**) gear system that turned a wheel just as a river would (see **Source B**). Factory owners started to notice when they realized they could power all their machines – by steam!

Factory fever!

The effect this had on Britain was incredible. Not only was steam power faster and more reliable, it also meant that factories no longer had to be built next to fast-flowing rivers – they could be built anywhere! Steam-powered factories started to spring up all over Britain and more and more people left the countryside to go and work in them. Factory towns like Birmingham, Sheffield, Manchester, Bolton and Bradford started to grow and grow. By 1850, Britain's factories produced two-thirds of the world's cotton cloth – even though cotton didn't grow in Britain! Nearly half of the world's hardware (tools, pots, pans and so on) also came from Britain. **Industry** had become **mechanized** and Britain was now known as 'the workshop of the world'. Also, for the first time in history, more people were now living in towns and cities than in the countryside!

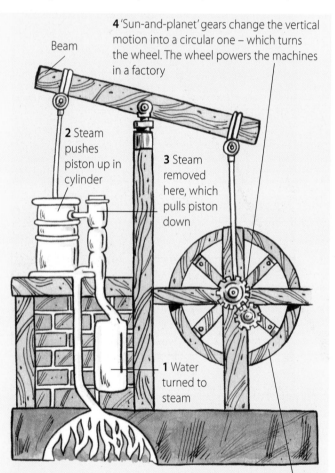

Beam

4 'Sun-and-planet' gears change the vertical motion into a circular one – which turns the wheel. The wheel powers the machines in a factory

2 Steam pushes piston up in cylinder

3 Steam removed here, which pulls piston down

1 Water turned to steam

Wheel attached to belts which drive factory machines

SOURCE B: *A steam engine's job is to turn a wheel. To do this, coal is burned to turn the water in the boiler into steam. This steam escapes into the cylinder and pushes up the piston – which in turn pushes up one end of the beam. When the piston reaches the top of the cylinder, the steam escapes and the piston – and beam – are allowed to fall back down. The whole process then begins again and the see-saw action of the beam is used to turn the wheel through the 'sun-and-planet' gears.*

Be a Top Historian

Top historians know when events, people and changes are **significant** – that is, when they change lots of people's lives. Can you identify any significant events, people or changes in Britain at this time?

'We look in astonishment as our coach drives on. The further we go, the more houses there are, collected along the road. All around we see flames, hissing and rattling. The windows of factories shaking as we go by. The sun darkens as if cloud has blocked it; suddenly it is evening on a bright day! As our horses stop, we see this is a dirty, evil-smelling town.'

SOURCE C: *Written by George Weerth, a German writer, living in Bradford, England, in 1840.*

SOURCE D: *Bradford after industrialization.*

Hungry for More?

The Lunar Society was a group of brilliant men who used to get together at Boulton's house in Birmingham to share and discuss ideas. They met once a month – on the Monday that was closest to the full moon – and were committed to using the new developments in science to improve people's lives. See if you can find out any more about the Lunar Society's members, ideas and innovations.

Work

1 **a** Read **Source A**. What type of power is used in this factory?
   b Name two problems that this type of power caused the factory owner.

2 Look at **Source B**. Write a sentence to explain the role of the following:
   • coal • piston • sun-and-planet gears • beam • boiler • wheel

3 Name two advantages that steam power had over water power for factory owners.

4 Read **Source C**. Do you think this source was written before or after Britain's industry had become mechanized? Give reasons for your answer.

5 Look at **Source D**.
   a How do you think the mills and factories of Bradford were powered? Explain your answer.
   b What negative effects does this form of power cause?

If you could visit one of Britain's early factories, perhaps the first thing you would notice would be the disgusting and dangerous working conditions. Most factory owners only cared about making a profit, not wasting money on providing a safe place to work. The machines were not fitted with any safety covers or guards and workers were not provided with goggles to protect their eyes. Factories were so noisy that people often went deaf and the dust made everyone sick. These hot, sweaty places would smell as well... the stench would come from overflowing toilet buckets at the end of each room!

Mission Objective

- Investigate what it was like to work in some of Britain's first factories.

Child labour

You would also notice a lot of children. Poor children didn't go to school, so boys and girls (some as young as five) would go to work with their parents. Other children working in the factories were **pauper apprentices**. They were often orphans who were sent to work in the factories by the authorities in the towns that were meant to look after them. In return for food, clothing and a bed in the 'apprentice house' next to the factory, the owners agreed to take care of the orphans, train them and 'keep them off the streets'. In reality, the factory practically owned them.

Now put yourself in the shoes of Peter, a pauper apprentice who worked in one of Britain's mills. While reading his story, ask yourself the question, 'Would you have been tough enough to survive?'

1 The apprentice house was usually just a short walk from the factory.

2 Some nasty factory owners advanced the factory clocks by 15 minutes in the morning so that all of the workers were late and were fined.

3 Some children spent years pulling and pushing heavy baskets, and their bodies became deformed as a result.

4 At about 8:00am there was a half-an-hour break.

FACT!

Poor children have always worked throughout history. They did jobs out on the farms like weeding and looking after animals. These jobs were boring but not particularly hard. In the factories life got much tougher!

Work

1 ✏ Write a sentence or two to explain these words:
   • overseer • pauper apprentice

I'm scared of Mr Willis, the overseer.

5 Overseers were factory managers who were given the job of making the children work as hard as possible. The more work the children did, the more the overseers were paid.

FACTORY RULES

1. Any worker late for work – 3d fine. They will not be let into the factory until breakfast time.
2. Any worker leaving the room without permission – 3d fine.
3. All broken brushes, oil cans, windows, wheels etc. will be paid for by the worker.
4. Any worker seen talking to another, heard whistling, singing or swearing – 6d fine.
5. Any worker who is ill and fails to find someone to do their jobs – 6d fine.

6 Factory rules were very strict. 6d was about half a day's pay for a woman.

This'll teach you not to work so slowly!

7 Workers weren't just fired or sacked for breaking rules – they were sometimes beaten with sticks or whipped.

8 A common punishment in one nail-making factory in the Midlands was to hammer a nail through the offender's ear into a wooden bench.

9 The workers would get between 30 minutes and an hour for dinner. In some factories, the pauper apprentices didn't get any plates – instead they just held out the bottom of their shirts and the cooks poured in the food.

Accidents are common here – none of the machines have covers or guards.

10 In 1833, two out of every five accident cases received at Manchester Infirmary were caused by factory machinery.

11 On average, pauper apprentices like Peter were smaller and lighter than boys and girls of a similar age who didn't work in factories.

12 They generally worked a 12-hour day, but at busy times of the year it could be as long as 14 or 15 hours.

13 Even the children who weren't orphans and lived with their parents earned about half the amount that women did… so it was cheaper for the factory owner to employ women and children over men.

14 Goods at the owner's shop were usually of poor quality – and the workers generally rented their house from the factory owners too!

15 When one group got in at the end of the day, the other crawled out of the same filthy sheets on the beds that they shared.

16 The pauper apprentices were owned by the factory until they were 21. Then they often got a job in the same factory.

SOURCE A: *A drawing showing an overseer about to punish a child.*

Inspector: Tell me boy, where do you live?
Child: 26 Duke Street, Leeds.
I: Do you work in the factories?
C: Yes, Sir.
I: At what age did you begin to work in them?
C: I was nearly eight years, I think.
I: How many hours a day do you work?
C: From six in the morning until seven at night.
I: Are you beaten at work?
C: Yes, Sir. If we look up from our work or speak to each other, we are beaten.
I: If you don't go as fast as the machines, are you beaten?
C: Yes, Sir. There's screaming among the boys and girls all day. They make black and blue marks on our bodies.
I: Are you allowed to 'make water' any time of the day?
C: No, only when a boy comes to tell you it's your turn. Whether you want to go or not, that's the only time you're allowed to go.
I: Can you hold your water for that long?
C: No, we're forced to let it go.
I: Do you spoil and wet yourself then?
C: Yes.

SOURCE B: *An inspector's report on children in factories. What do you think is meant by the phrase 'make water'?*

FACT!

Some factory owners had been trying to help their workers for years. Robert Owen built quality houses, schools, shops with cheap goods, and parks for his workers in Scotland. He even reduced working hours. He believed that happy workers made hard workers – and he was rewarded with huge profits!

What Happened When?

1824

The Society for the Prevention of Cruelty to Animals (now the RSPCA) was set up in 1824. At this time, animals seemed to have had more protection than the pauper apprentices!

Work

1 a Make your own 24-hour timeline for a typical weekday in your life today. Be careful to include:
  - all your sleep time
  - times for food, travel, breaks and any spare time
  - what work you do (a paper round perhaps).

NOTE: You will also have to include something that a factory boy or girl wouldn't have done… school!

b Write at least five sentences, each one stating how your day is different (or similar) to a child's in 1820.

c Why do you think the treatment of children in Britain has changed so much? Explain your answer carefully – you are being asked for your opinion here.

2 🖊 The Big Write!

Imagine you have been given the job of carrying out a factory inspection. Write a report for the government based on the information on pages 22–25.

Include the following sections:
- An introduction – addressed to the audience of your report
- Dangerous and unhealthy conditions – What accidents have you heard about? Why are some children deformed? What diseases and illnesses do workers catch?
- Cruelty and punishments – How are rule breakers treated? Are punishments appropriate?
- The future – Why do some owners seem unwilling to make their factories safer? What improvements could be made?

You could include an interview with a factory owner and/or a worker, written out like a play script, and a picture or diagram to illustrate your points.

Remember, reports should use formal language, and be structured with headings.

What was 'black gold'?

Coal is a hard, black rock that is buried underground. Once it is lit, it burns for a long time – much longer than wood. At the start of the eighteenth century, Britain had a lot of coal in many areas. It was very cheap and was used mainly to cook with and heat houses. The workers that got the coal out of the ground – **miners** – didn't have to dig very deep to get at it at first. They got all they needed from large pits near the surface. So why did the demand for coal suddenly increase? Why did coal mining turn into one of the country's most dangerous jobs? And why did some people start to refer to coal as 'black gold'?

More coal!

After 1745, more coal was needed… much, much more! There were many people with homes to heat and food to cook for a start. It was also needed to power steam engines in new factories that were springing up all over the country and was used in the making of bricks, pottery, glass, beer, sugar, soap and iron. Coal was also required to power the steam trains that travelled across the country and steam ships that sailed the seas. And the need for more coal meant more money for the mine owners. In fact, some mine owners were making so much money from their coal that they began to refer to it as 'black gold'.

Deeper and deeper

Although the demand for coal meant more money for mine owners, soon the coal near to the surface began to run out – so the miners had to dig deeper and deeper underground to get it.

SOURCE A: *The coalfields of Britain in 1800.*

Causes of Death	Age		
	Under 13	13–18	18+
Gas explosion	12	21	43
Gunpowder explosion	1	0	1
Crushed	0	0	3
Suffocated (by choke damp)	3	0	8
Drowned	8	3	9
Hit by falling coal, stones and rubbish	23	20	55
Fall from the shafts	7	15	35
Fall from the rope breaking	0	2	3
Fall when ascending	2	2	6
Hit by wagons	5	3	9
Drawn over the pulley	5	2	3
Injuries in coal mines (unspecified)	10	6	25
Total	76	74	200

SOURCE B: *Causes of death in a Yorkshire mine, 1805.*

'Because of the water, the filth and the heat, men, women and children often worked stark naked in the slushy, black mud in the dark tunnels. It is little wonder that they lived like animals below ground, and often little better when they reached the surface… working 12 or more hours under the ground, and going down before dawn and coming up after dark, many saw daylight only on Sunday.'

▲ **SOURCE C:** *A modern historian, Peter Moss, describes a miner's life,* History Alive 3, 1789–1914.

Daniel's story

As the mines got deeper, the work got harder. In fact, mining was one of the most dangerous jobs in the country. Read the following diary entry carefully. It outlines a typical day for Daniel Douglas, a 15-year-old boy in a Welsh mine.

14 August 1839

What a day! I'm on the night shift this week, so I have to get to the cage at six in the evening. This mine is one of the deepest around here – 500 metres – but the drop to the bottom only takes about half a minute. The trip in the lift is dark, noisy and very scary.

Far from fresh air and daylight, I start to 'walk out'. The 6km walk to the coalface takes forever. By the time I actually start working, I've been down the pit for over an hour!

After hanging up my safety lamp (it burns brighter if there's any poisonous gas about), I light a candle for a bit of extra glow and start to dig. Using my pick and shovel, chisels and hammers, I knock out lumps of coal from the seam. The coal lies in these seams, or layers, between ordinary rock. I pull out the coal and throw it into a large, strong sack. Young girls called bearers take our sacks away from the coalface and put the lumps of coal into wagons. For all of us, work in the mines is torture – swollen knees, bruised ribs, broken fingers and bleeding heads. The coal dust makes us cough and vomit.

After eight hours it's time to make my way back up to the surface. I always have a chat with some of the trappers on my way out because it was the job I used to do when I first started working here ten years ago. Those little children open and close trapdoors to let the coal wagons pass by on the underground tracks. Drawers push and pull the loaded wagons towards the lifts that take them up to the surface.

When they're not taking any coal up, the lifts take us back up to the surface – about 11 hours after I first started! It's daylight when I finish work. The mine never closes and it must be making the owner a fortune. No wonder they've started to call coal 'black gold'.

Before I collapse into bed, I eat before falling into a very deep sleep. I'll be back at the lift later this evening when it starts all over again.

Time for change?

As you can see, conditions in the mines were very poor – and eventually the government took notice of this. A report on mining was published in 1842 and the interviews, information and pictures shocked people. Soon, new laws were introduced banning women and children under ten from working in mines. Inspectors were appointed too. Now these small changes certainly didn't make mining a much safer job… but it was a move in the right direction!

Work

1 After 1745, why were deeper mines needed?

2 What were the dangers involved in mining? **Sources B** and **C** will help you.

3 Read Daniel Douglas' diary entry carefully.
   a At what age did he begin working down the mine?
   b Explain carefully what Daniel used to do when he first started to work in the mine.
   c What did 'bearers' and 'drawers' do?
   d Why might Daniel be able to see daylight when he was trying to get to sleep after work?
   e According to Daniel, why is the mine owner making so much money?

The eighteenth century saw major advances in the use and production of iron. It had been produced in Britain since Roman times but in the 1700s it began to be used in all areas of life. The army used it for cannons, the navy for 'iron-clad' ships, and the new factories were held up with iron girders and used iron machines that were powered by iron steam engines! It was used to make tools, trains and their tracks, and at home people sat around fireplaces with iron grates and cooked on iron stoves using iron pans. So how was iron made? How was this process improved? And who went 'iron mad' in this new 'Age of iron'?

Mission Objectives

- Discover how iron was produced.
- Investigate how iron-making became such an important business.

So, how is iron actually made? Read through cartoons 1–4 to find out:

1 Iron ore is dug from the ground. Iron ore is a rock from which iron, a type of metal, can be removed.

2 The ore is then melted together with limestone (to remove impurities) and charcoal (baked wood) in a furnace. Huge bellows 'blast' air in to raise the temperature. The metal (iron) gets so hot it melts and pours out of the bottom of the furnace.

3 Red-hot, liquid iron is then poured into casts shaped like pots, pans, pipes, cannons, beams and so on. **Cast iron** is strong but contains air bubbles that can make it brittle.

4 When cast iron is reheated and hammered, the pockets of air are removed and it becomes **wrought iron**. This is purer, stronger, more bendy and is used for chains, tools, furniture, train tracks and so on.

SOURCE A: *How to make iron in the 1700s.*

The kings of Coalbrookdale!

As the population and the number of factories grew, so did the demand for iron. But the producers of iron faced a problem – Britain was running out of forests! Charcoal (made from wood) was needed to make the iron, and charcoal was getting harder to find. It was possible to use coal, instead of charcoal, to make iron, but coal contains too much sulphur (a chemical) and makes poor quality iron. Luckily for Britain, a family called the Darbys got involved in the iron industry!

> In 1709 I discovered a way of using coal to make iron! All you need to do is heat it first in order to remove the sulphur. This makes something called coke (not the drink!). Cast iron made with coke is much better quality than cast iron made with coal – iron production could continue!

Abraham Darby I, 1678–1717

> I improved the process invented by my father, removing even more impurities and allowing wrought iron to be made from coke-fired coal!

Abraham Darby II, 1711–1763

Abraham Darby III, 1750–1789

> I carried on the good work of my father and grandfather and decided to show what is possible using their iron with this magnificent iron bridge! Now our ironworks at Coalbrookdale is famous throughout the world!

Ironbridge – one of the wonders of the world!

The iron bridge over the River Severn at Coalbrookdale, Shropshire, was a massive success. When it opened on New Year's Day 1781, it caused a sensation. Writers, artists and rich tourists came from all over the world to see this modern miracle – and Darby charged every one of them to walk across it! It was also a fantastic advertisement for what could be achieved with iron, and iron production became one of Britain's most important industries (see **Source B**). No wonder people began to call the period the 'Age of iron'.

Year	How much was produced in Britain?
1745	30,000 tons
1800	250,000 tons
1850	2,000,000 tons
1901	6,000,000 tons

SOURCE B: *Iron produced in Britain 1745–1901. After 1856, steel (made from iron) started to be produced in Britain, too.*

Work

1 Using no more than three sentences, explain how iron is produced.

2 Explain the difference between cast iron and wrought iron.

3 Explain why Abraham Darby I was so important in increasing Britain's iron production.

4 Copy and complete the following paragraph:

The most famous iron makers of them all were the _____ family from _____, Shropshire. Their _____ was one of the finest in the world. One member of the family was so keen to show his iron off, he built the world's first _____ _____ over the River _____.

5 a Look at **Source B**. Draw a bar chart to show how Britain's iron production increased.
  b Write a description to accompany the chart, explaining the increase.

6 List three iron items that were essential for Britain's industry to become mechanized.

FACT!

It wasn't just the Darbys who were obsessed with finding new uses for iron. John 'iron mad' Wilkinson built an iron barge in 1787 and, later, built an iron church for his workers. When he died, he was even buried in an iron coffin under an iron monument!

The end of the 'Cripple Factory'

In 1800, a factory in Manchester was given a terrifying nickname. It was known as the 'Cripple Factory'. Years and years of heavy lifting, broken arms and severe beatings meant that many of the young men, women and children who worked there were crippled forever. The mines weren't much better either. One 11-year-old girl working as a coal-carrier describes her job in **Source A**. **Source B** also gives an idea of what her job entailed.

Mission Objectives

- Identify why some factory owners were unwilling to improve working conditions.
- Select three key reforms that eventually improved life for Britain's workers.

Time to reform

Today, the British government would not let this sort of thing happen. Many people in 1800 thought that politicians had no right to interfere with the working conditions in factories. They believed that it was up to the owners to decide how they ran their factories and mines. After all, they owned them, didn't they?

However, others argued that people might work harder if they were treated better! **Reformers** like Lord Shaftesbury, Richard Oastler, John Fielden and Michael Sadler began to campaign for laws to protect the men, women and children who worked in the factories and mines. Some of these people collected evidence to prove how bad things were. Their findings shocked the nation. **Sources C** and **D** have been taken from two of the investigations and reports.

'I go down the pit at two in the morning and I don't come up again until the next afternoon. I go to bed at six at night to be ready for work the next morning... I carry coal tubs up ladders all day. Each coal tub holds $4^{1}/_{4}$ cwt* [216 kg – about as heavy as three adults] and I get beaten when I don't work hard enough.'

SOURCE A: *A worker describes working in a mine, 1842. (*cwt = hundredweight)*

Interviewer: Were you sometimes late?

Joseph: Yes, and if we were even five minutes late, we were beaten black and blue by the overseer. He hit us with a strap.

Interviewer: Do you know of any accidents?

Joseph: Yes, there was a boy who got hit by a machine. He broke both legs and one of them was cut open from his knee to his waist. His head was cut, his eyes were nearly torn out and he broke both arms.

SOURCE C: *A few questions and answers from the Sadler Report, an investigation into factory conditions in 1832 by an MP called Michael Sadler. Dozens of workers like Joseph Hebergram were interviewed. WARNING: Some historians think Sadler exaggerated the answers when writing up his investigations. He wanted conditions to appear even worse than they already were. Regardless of this, the Sadler Report made a huge impact.*

SOURCE B: *An 1842 illustration of a girl bent over carrying coal.*

'I have a belt around my waist... and I go on my hands and feet... the belt and chain are worse when we are in the family way [pregnant].'
'I've had three or four children born on the same days as I have been at work and have gone back to work nine or ten days later. Four out of my eight children were still-born.'

SOURCE D: *From the mines report of 1842, based on interviews with two women, Mary Hardman and Betty Harris (who pulled coal along in large wagons).*

Change is coming

After reading the reports, Parliament acted. From 1833, new laws or Acts made great changes to the working lives of women and children. Men, it was believed, could look after themselves.

Some factory owners hated the changes. They felt politicians had no right to interfere in their business and thought of ways to avoid keeping to the new rules. But the new laws kept coming and, gradually, they began to protect more and more workers. Inspectors were even appointed to enforce them! By 1900, factories and mines had become safer and more bearable. They still weren't particularly pleasant places to work but Parliament had accepted that they had a duty to look after the more vulnerable people in society.

1833 FACTORY ACT
– No children under nine to work in the factories.
– Nine hours of work per day for children aged nine to thirteen.
– Two hours of school per day.
– Factory inspectors appointed (but there were only four!).

1842 MINES ACT
– No women or children under ten to work down a mine.
– Mine inspectors appointed.

1847 TEN HOUR ACT
– Maximum ten-hour day for all women and workers under 18.

1844 FACTORY ACT
– No women to work more than 12 hours per day.
– Machines to be made safer.

1850 FACTORY ACT
– Machines to only be operated by women and children between 6:00am and 6:00pm.

1871 TRADE UNION ACT
– Trade unions made legal. Workers all doing the same job (trade) – like railway workers or dockers, for example – were allowed to join together (unionize) to negotiate with their employers for improvements to pay and working conditions. As a last resort, all union members could go on strike!

1895 FACTORY ACT
– Children under 13 to work a maximum of 30 hours per week.

SOURCE E: *New acts to protect workers.*

Wise Up Words
reformer

Work

1 **a** How did the 'Cripple Factory' get its terrifying nickname?

   b In your opinion, were the mines just as bad as some factories? Support your answer using evidence from some of the sources.

2 **a** Explain the word 'reformer'.

   b How did reformers bring about changes to working conditions?

3 Look at **Source C**.

   a Write down three words or phrases that a reader of this report might feel.

   b Why might this interview NOT be totally reliable? Give reasons for your answer.

   c Do any of Joseph's answers seem a bit exaggerated? Explain your answer.

   d How could a historian get a more reliable view of factory life in the 1800s? You might want to discuss this question with your classmates or teacher.

4 Look at **Source E**.

   a Write down what you think are three of the most important changes to working conditions between 1830 and 1895.

   b Next to each one, explain why you think it was an important change.

Turnpike fever!

Take two of Britain's most important cities: London and Edinburgh. The distance between them is about 675km and if you travelled from one city to the other in 1745, it would have taken you a week by boat or two weeks by road. That's right – two whole weeks of travelling to get there! By 1901, you could make the same journey in just nine hours! So how was this improvement possible?

Mission Objectives

- Outline the problems with Britain's transport system in 1745.
- Assess how Britain's roads were improved.

Hit the road, Jack!

In 1745, Britain's roads were in a sorry state. They always had been but they were now busier than ever. Coal had to be taken from the mines to the factories and then to the towns, in order to heat people's homes. Cotton also had to be moved from the ports to the factories before the finished goods had to be moved to market. A fast and reliable postal service was needed for businessmen too. Many people used the sea or rivers to get around – especially when moving heavy goods like iron or coal – but dozens of towns were miles from the nearest river. For them, the only alternative was to take to the road – and they met a host of problems!

Stand and deliver!

Britain's roads were lonely, isolated places that were completely unlit at night. As soon as travellers left the safety of the towns, they were sitting targets for robbers and bandits, known as **highwaymen**. With no hope of sending for help, passengers in a **stagecoach** often found themselves handing over valuables while looking down the barrel of a gun!

The rocky road to ruin

Even if you weren't the victim of an armed robbery, Britain's roads were still dangerous places. They were so rutted and full of huge potholes that coaches often became stuck or had their wheels smashed. Some of the potholes were so big that people actually drowned in them! Every male villager was supposed to spend six days each year repairing the roads, but as they rarely left their fields, the roads got worse and worse the further away you got from the village.

SOURCE A: *Written by Arthur Young, a traveller.*

'Let me warn all travellers... to avoid this road like the devil... They will meet here with ruts, which actually measured four feet deep and floating with mud in the summer. What can it be like in winter?... I passed three carts broken down in 18 miles.'

SOURCE B: *A painting entitled* The Mishap, *1806. Travelling by Britain's roads might have been very slow but it was still extremely dangerous!*

Time for the turnpikes!

The government could see businesses were losing money because of the terrible roads and decided to act. They divided Britain's main roads up and rented each section to a group called a '**turnpike trust**'. These groups promised to improve their road and maintain it. In return, trusts were allowed to charge a **toll** to every person that used their section of road. Turnpike roads had gates at the end of each stretch where toll keepers collected the money. Much of the cash was used to improve the roads and specialist engineers went on to create the finest roads Britain had ever seen.

By 1830, there were nearly 1000 turnpike trusts improving over 32,000km of roads, to dramatic effect. It might have taken you two weeks to travel from London to Edinburgh in 1745 – but by 1830 you could get there in about 48 hours!

What Happened When?

After George IV died, his brother William IV became king, in 1830.

Wise Up Words

highwayman   stagecoach   toll
toll keeper   turnpike trust

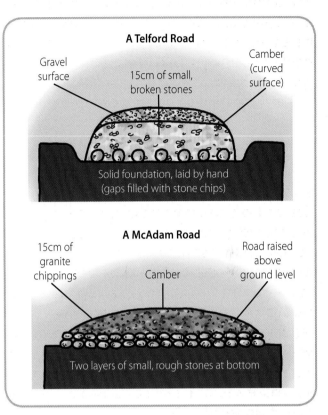

A Telford Road

Gravel surface

15cm of small, broken stones

Camber (curved surface)

Solid foundation, laid by hand (gaps filled with stone chips)

A McAdam Road

15cm of granite chippings

Camber

Road raised above ground level

Two layers of small, rough stones at bottom

SOURCE C: *Thomas Telford and John McAdam were Britain's most famous road builders. McAdam's roads were most popular – they were cheaper – and hundreds of trusts paid for 'McAdamised' roads. Years later, tar was added to the surface and it became known as 'tarmac'.*

Work

1 a How long did it take to get from London to Edinburgh by road in 1745?

b Why do you think the journey took so long? Use **Sources A** and **B** to explain your answer.

c Why didn't more people use water transport instead of the roads?

2 a Match the names in **List A** with the descriptions in **List B**:

List A	List B
turnpike trust	a small fee or tax paid for using the road
turnpike road	a group of businessmen, responsible for improving a stretch of road and keeping it in good order
toll	collects tolls at the start of the journey
toll keeper	a road controlled by a turnpike trust

b Read this list of people:
- farmers
- the army
- the Post Office
- factory owners
- businessmen
- horse and coach companies.

Decide which groups benefited from better roads. In each case, give reasons why they benefited.

3 Look at **Source C**.

a In what ways are these roads better than the road described in **Source A**?

b By 1830, how long did it take to get from London to Edinburgh?

Canal mania!

The turnpikes had given Britain some of the best roads in the world and journey times had been made much shorter – but many businessmen still weren't happy. They were convinced that their profits could be increased if a different form of transport was used. So what were the problems with the new roads? What solution did they come up with? And was this the answer to Britain's transport problems?

Mission Objectives

- Discover why turnpike roads weren't suitable for some businessmen.
- Define what a canal is and justify why the Duke of Bridgewater built one.
- Propose two reasons why 'canal mania' ended.

Warning! Wide load!

The growth of towns and the number of factories meant that roads were busier than ever. But it wasn't just the number of vehicles on the roads that caused businessmen headaches – it was the things they were carrying. Factories needed a constant supply of coal, and the new ironworks were delivering huge, heavy objects all over the country. This was a lot for a poor horse to drag – especially uphill!

Bridgewater's brains!

The Duke of Bridgewater owned coal mines in Worsley. Although there was a great demand for his coal just 14km away in Manchester, he couldn't get it there quick enough. It was also costing him a fortune in tolls as the horses and carts had to pay every time they made the journey. Bridgewater realized that if he built an inland waterway between Manchester and his mines, not only would he avoid the tolls, he could move – and sell – a lot more coal! He borrowed a fortune and turned to a brilliant engineer called James Brindley to cut him Britain's first industrial **canal**.

Brilliant Brindley!

A canal is a long, narrow, man-made channel of still water – a bit like a giant, long bath! It has to remain completely level all the way along or the water would flow downhill and empty the canal. Unfortunately for Bridgewater, the River Irwell and its steep valley ran right across the path of his canal. He had to think of a way of getting boats across this valley – and his solution was Britain's first **aqueduct** of its kind. This basically carried the canal over the valley on legs and was described as the 'most extraordinary thing in the kingdom, if not in Europe'.

What a smashing idea!

Another businessman, Josiah Wedgwood, decided he wanted a canal for different reasons. Wedgwood had cashed in on the popularity of tea drinking and had a thriving business making thousands of cups, saucers and teapots at his pottery in Stoke-on-Trent. Yet he was not making as much money as he could have because some of his goods were being smashed on their bumpy journey to the market. Canal barges guaranteed a much smoother ride than any road and more of Wedgwood's delicate china was soon reaching his customers in one piece.

SOURCE A: *The Bridgewater Canal opened on 17 July 1761 and was an instant success. It might have cost a fortune to build but the Duke's coal got to Manchester twice as fast and for half the price of road travel!*

Canal crazy!

As canals were ideal for moving heavy goods like coal and iron, and perfect for moving fragile, breakable goods like pottery, they soon caught on. By 1830, 4000 miles of canal had been built and it was possible to travel to every major town and city in England by barge. 'Canal mania' provided work for thousands of **navvies** (the men who built them) as they all had to be dug out by hand.

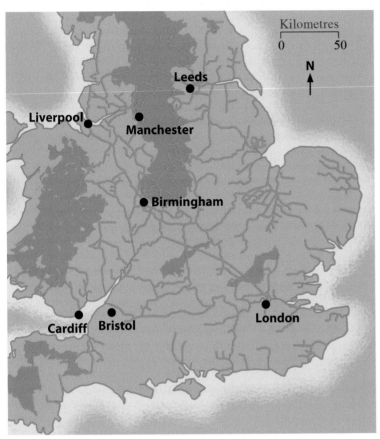

SOURCE B: *Britain's canal network. Soon every town in England could be reached by canal.*

Locked up!

Not every canal builder used aqueducts to get up and down hills – many decided to use canal locks. These are gated boxes that help to control the water level of the canal by allowing different amounts of water to pass through. It wasn't as quick as an aqueduct or tunnel but it was cheaper to build and got the job done!

The great age of canal building did not last long. They were too slow to transport mail (fast mail coaches could carry light items quicker), and they could freeze up in winter and dry out in summer. There wasn't really any passenger service on the canals either but, by the 1830s, inventors had come up with a new form of transport. Britain was entering the age of the train!

Wise Up Words

aqueduct   canal   navvy   transported

FACT!

In 1842, William John Shaw, aged 16, stole a man's clothes while he was taking a dip in a canal. He was soon caught, and was **transported** for seven years on a convict ship!

Work

1   Use all the information on pages 34 and 35:
   a   Make a list of all the reasons why roads were not suitable for some people.
   b   Make another list of reasons why canals were useful to Bridgewater, Wedgwood and other businessmen.
   c   Make a final list which shows some of the problems associated with canals.

2   What do you think the phrase 'canal mania' means? Explain your answer fully.

3   In your own words, explain how canals moved up and down hills.

SOURCE C: *Locks allowed barges to move up and down hill.*

When steam engines first appeared in the 1700s, inventors wondered whether steam power could be used for turning wheels. If it could, surely the invention of the **locomotive** – a steam engine that moved wheels along a set of rails – was not far away. By 1800, the race was on to build a safe and reliable steam locomotive.

Mission Objectives

- Explain what is meant by the word 'locomotive'.
- Assess the importance of the Liverpool and Manchester Railway.

Do the locomotion!

The man credited with building the world's first railway locomotive was a Cornishman called Richard Trevithick. In 1804, to win a bet, his engine pulled ten tons of iron and 70 passengers for 14.5km in Merthyr Tydfil, South Wales. The passengers called his big, metal engine an 'iron horse'. The journey took four hours and many at the time said it would have been quicker if they had walked! Nevertheless, it was a historic journey.

Four years later, he raced his new locomotive – *Catch Me Who Can* – against horses on a round track on the site of what is now Euston Station in London. He charged passengers 5p for a ride.

SOURCE A: *The* Catch Me Who Can *of 1808. Trevithick was a clever engineer, but not a good businessman. He died a poor man in 1833.*

Copy cats

Other engineers saw their chance to make money too. One of them was George Stephenson, who built his first locomotive – the *Blücher* – in 1814. It pulled coal (very slowly) at his local mine, Killingworth Colliery, near Newcastle upon Tyne.

In 1821, Stephenson was asked to build a 32km rail track from the port of Stockton on Tees to a coal mine in Darlington. The promoter of the railway, Edward Pease, intended to use horses to pull carts full of coal along the track, but Stephenson persuaded him to use one of his steam locomotives instead. On 27 September 1825, Stephenson's *Active* pulled 12 wagons full of coal, a coach and 21 passenger cars at the opening of the Stockton and Darlington Railway. This was the first public transport system in the world to use steam locomotives. Some passengers fainted when the train reached the speed of 12 miles per hour – they were absolutely terrified!

A new railway line

A year later, Stephenson was given a much bigger job. He was asked to plan and build the first railway line between major cities: Liverpool and Manchester. The railway would run for 48km, include a huge tunnel, 63 bridges, and a **viaduct** across a river. Stephenson went straight to work and by 1829 the line was nearing completion.

In October 1829, a contest was arranged at Rainhill, near Liverpool, to see if any engineer could design a safe and reliable engine to use on the new railway. Four men entered their locomotives, including Stephenson with his engine called the *Rocket*, which he had built with his son, Robert.

The Rainhill Trials

A huge crowd turned up to watch the contestants race their engines on a 3km length of track. As well as Stephenson, the owners of three other steam engines – the *Sans Pareil*, the *Novelty* and the *Perseverance* – were all keen to get their hands on the £500 prize (see **Sources B** and **C**).

As **Source C** states, the *Rocket* easily outperformed the others and was declared the winner. And a year later the *Rocket* was used on the opening day of the new Liverpool and Manchester Railway.

A railway to die for

The Liverpool and Manchester Railway opened on 15 September 1830 with the Prime Minister and old war hero the Duke of Wellington as guest of honour. Huge crowds gathered to watch and grandstands were built specially. But it wasn't the best of starts, especially for the MP for Liverpool, William Huskisson, who was run over by the *Rocket* and died of his injuries later that day. And despite this tragedy, they tried to continue with the ceremony… but the locomotive broke down! It even took Wellington six hours to get back to Manchester.

A roaring success

Despite the tragic opening, the railway was a huge success. By December, dozens of trains were carrying passengers, coal, timber, cattle, sheep and pigs between the two cities. By 1831, the railway was taking over £200,000 each year in fares. And it was only taking just over an hour to get from Liverpool to Manchester, much faster than road or canal. Without a doubt, the 'railway age' had begun.

SOURCE B: *The Rainhill Trials of 1829, featuring Stephenson's* Rocket.

Dear James   16 October 1829

We have just finished the contest and the *Rocket* has been triumphant. We will take hold of the £500. The *Rocket* is the best engine I have ever seen. The *Sans Pareil* burns a lot of fuel and mumbles and roars and rolls about like an empty beer barrel on a rough pavement. She is very ugly too. The *Novelty* seemed to dart away like a greyhound for a bit but wasn't reliable – always something exploding or blowing up. The *Perseverance* was last of all to start and was slow and noisy – as noisy as a pair of wicker baskets on an old donkey!

SOURCE C: *Based on a letter written by one of Stephenson's assistants after the contest.*

Work

1 Explain what is meant by the word 'locomotive'.

2 Each of these dates is important in railway history:
   - 1814
   - 1825
   - 1804
   - 1830
   - 1821
   - 1826
   - 1808
   - 1829
   a Put the dates in chronological order on separate lines in your book.
   b Beside each date, write what happened in that year in your own words.

3 Read **Source C**.
   a Why were the Rainhill Trials taking place?
   b Why did the *Rocket* win the trial?

4 **The Big Write!**

   Write a newspaper report for 16 September 1830 – the day after the opening of the railway. Your story must include: an eye-catching headline, details of what happened on the opening day, details of the locomotive and how it was chosen, and what was special about the new railway. You might want to include a picture too. Remember, newspaper reports begin with the main facts – the '5Ws' – who, what, where, when, and why.

2.4 Train reaction!

By the 1850s, hundreds of kilometres of train track had been built all over Britain, and train travel had become an everyday event for thousands of people. The stagecoach and canal companies just could not compete with the speed, price and pulling power of the locomotives and many soon went out of business. But, unlike the improvements to the roads and the digging of the canals, the building of the railways didn't just benefit businessmen – they affected lots of other people too. So who else felt the benefit of the railways? What changes did they cause? And which consequence was the most important?

Mission Objectives

- Outline several examples of how the railways changed life in Britain.
- Judge which was most important and explain why.

CONSEQUENCE A:

'The traveller will live double time. By completing a distance in two hours that used to require four, he will have the other two at his disposal. The man of business in Manchester will breakfast at home, go to Liverpool by railway, complete his business and return to Manchester for dinner.'

H. Booth, 1830.

SOURCE A: *A map showing the railway network in 1852. Soon, every major town, city and port was linked.*

CONSEQUENCE B:

By 1880, about 300,000 people worked in jobs that depended on the railway. Iron, steel, bricks and timber were needed in huge quantities to build all the things the railways needed – locomotives, trucks, carriages, rails, sleepers, stations and so on. Miners were kept busy too, as a journey of 160km used about one ton of coal. Large numbers of men were also needed as rail workers too – guards, drivers, mechanics, maintenance and so on.

CONSEQUENCE C:

Before the railways, what time you set your watch to depended on where in the country you were. Midday was measured when the sun was at its highest point in the sky – but this was different in every city. Clocks in Reading were four minutes ahead of those in London, while clocks in Bristol were 11 minutes behind! As the trains ran between cities, this made timetables very complicated. As a result, in 1880, the whole country began to use the time set in Greenwich (London) and **Greenwich Mean Time (GMT)** was adopted.

CONSEQUENCE D:

'The district through which the railway passes is rich in coal and iron. Without the introduction of the railways into this part of Scotland, the valuable raw materials would have remained in the ground.'

A Scottish writer, 1842.

(Map labels: Glasgow, Kilmarnock, Ayr, Berwick, Newcastle, Carlisle, Whitehaven, Middlesborough, Whitby, Scarborough, Barrow in Furness, Skipton, York, Bradford, Leeds, Hull, Woodhead, Doncaster, Holyhead, Liverpool, Manchester, Sheffield, Gainsborough, Caernarfon, Chester, Derby, Newark, Lincoln, Nottingham, Trent, Shrewsbury, Stafford, Leicester, Peterborough, Norwich, Yarmouth, Birmingham, Ely, Ipswich, Carmarthen, Oxford, Colchester, Cardiff, Swindon, Reading, LONDON, Chippenham, Bristol, Salisbury, Ashford, Deal, Exeter, Dorchester, Southampton, Bodmin, Portsmouth, Brighton, Plymouth, N, 0 100km)

CONSEQUENCE E:

The railways changed what people ate. Fresh vegetables and dairy products could be moved from the farms into the city before they went off. The ability to get fresh fish in the cities meant pigs' trotters were soon replaced by fish and chips as the number one takeaway food!

CONSEQUENCE F:

In 1841, Crewe was a tiny village of 203 people. A major railway junction was built there and just 30 years later it had grown into a major town with a population of 18,000 people!

COME AND JOIN THE CREWE

CONSEQUENCE G:

High speed travel meant that sports clubs could now play teams from other towns in 'away' games. The Football League, which was formed in 1888 with 12 teams from all over the country, would never have been possible without the trains. Watching cricket and going to race meetings also became much more popular.

CONSEQUENCE H:

During the 1840s, Thomas Cook began organizing cheap day trains to the seaside. The British tradition of 'a day at the seaside' was born! Towns such as Blackpool, Brighton and Margate quickly grew and soon had hotels, piers and funfairs for the holidaymakers.

By 1901, there were over 32,000km of train track that carried millions of passengers every year. London even had its own underground railway – or 'Tube' – that took workers from the growing **suburbs** into the city. It all had an amazing effect on journey time. Indeed, a journey between London and Edinburgh took two weeks by road in 1745. By 1901, you could make that journey in nine hours – thanks to the railway!

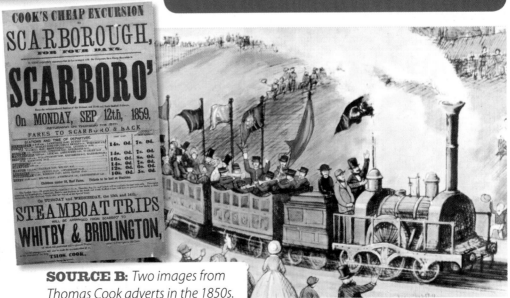

SOURCE B: *Two images from Thomas Cook adverts in the 1850s.*

Work

1   Copy out the subtitles below. For each one, write a sentence or two explaining how the railways changed this area of life:
   - Sport
   - Time
   - Diet
   - Holidays
   - Employment
   - Town creation
   - **Commuting**
   - Raw materials.

2   List the changes in the order that you think were most important. Write a paragraph explaining the choices you have made.

Be a Top Historian

Top historians can spot when an event or a change is **significant**. This means it has a huge impact in lots of ways on lots of people. Can you explain the **significance** of the invention of railways?

Between 1745 and 1901, the British were a very inventive lot! They designed new ways to do things that no one had ever thought of before. New machines did things better, faster and for longer. Then they were redesigned and further improved. Some of Britain's greatest inventors and designers lived during this time and, as a result, Britain's technology became the envy of the world. You've got eight nominees to choose from, each one an important figure in Britain's gradual emergence as the 'workshop of the world' and the 'hotbed of invention'. Now it's up to you to decide who the most important figure was during this time.

Mission Objectives

- Identify some of the achievements of Britain's great inventors, designers and scientists.
- Judge who you think deserves the title 'Greatest Inventor and/or Designer'.

I'd like to extend a warm welcome to all the students out there lucky enough to get one of the best seats in the house for tonight's award show. Like many awards, the decision will be made by you! Based on the evidence presented to you, you must choose the person who deserves the title 'Greatest Inventor and/or Designer'.

Be a Top Historian

You are about to discover things about some very **significant** people. For each person, think:

- Why were they important?
- How did they change things?
- Are they more important than any of the other people?

Meet the nominees!

Richard Arkwright.

James Watt.

George Stephenson.

Michael Faraday.

Isambard Kingdom Brunel.

Henry Bessemer.

Alexander Graham Bell.

Charles Babbage.

Nominee No. 1: Richard Arkwright
Nickname: The father of the factory system

- Born in Preston in 1732.

- Early jobs included hairdressing and wig making.

- Invented a new spinning machine that could make thick, strong thread very fast, much faster than any other machine.

- Built factories to house these large spinning machines.

- Opened Britain's first steam-powered cotton factory (in Cromford, Derbyshire). By 1813, there were over 2000 steam-driven spinning machines in Britain producing cloth worth £40 million! To some, he was 'the father of the factory system'.

- His factories employed thousands of people.

- After being knighted in 1786, he still felt he wasn't clever enough to be worthy of the title 'Sir Richard'. He sat down every day to improve his reading, writing and spelling.

Supporter No. 1: The modern historians Paul Shuter and John Child, in *The Changing Face of Britain*

'Richard Arkwright… was certainly a great entrepreneur. He had faith in the inventions, he risked his money and persuaded other people to risk theirs. He got very rich in the process… Without the inventors, industry as we know it could not have started. Without entrepreneurs, it could not have developed. They decided which risks to take. When they were successful, they laid the foundations for our industry today.'

Supporter No. 2: The modern historian J F Aylett, from *In Search of History, 1714–1900*

'But Arkwright was a clever businessman… in the mill; thousands of spindles were all spinning thread at once. By his death [in 1792] Arkwright was running ten mills; he had made himself a fortune of £500,000. And the factory age had arrived.'

Wise Up Words

rotary motion   water frame

SOURCE A: *Richard Arkwright.*

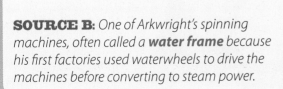

SOURCE B: *One of Arkwright's spinning machines, often called a **water frame** because his first factories used waterwheels to drive the machines before converting to steam power.*

Nominee No. 2: James Watt
Nickname: Mr Power

- Born in Greenock, Scotland, in 1736. He worked as an instrument maker at the University of Glasgow.

- In 1764, Watt was asked to repair an old steam engine. These engines were used mainly in mines to pump out water, but were slow and kept breaking down. They only produced an 'up and down' motion, but were useful for pumping water out of mines.

- Watt greatly improved the older steam engine. He made it faster and more reliable. It used less coal too!

- In 1781, Watt designed a steam engine that could turn a wheel. This is called **rotary motion**. Now steam power could be used to drive machinery.

- By 1800, Watt and Boulton's factory in Birmingham was producing some of the finest steam engines in the world. Gradually, steam power replaced horse, water, wind and muscle power.

Supporter: By modern historian Bea Stimpson, in *The World of Empire, Industry and Trade*

'… by 1800, there were nearly 500 Boulton and Watt steam engines in use. This machine, by replacing hand and muscle power in many industries, transformed the lives of hundreds of thousands of workers.'

SOURCE A: *In 2011, James Watt (right) and his business partner Matthew Boulton (left) appeared on a £50 note. The famous steam engine Watt designed appears on the note too.*

Nominee No. 3: George Stephenson
Nickname: The father of the railways

- First job at 14 was working at the local coal mine with his father.

- Designed his first steam locomotive, the *Blücher*, in 1814 – but it was no quicker than using horses to pull coal wagons.

- In 1815, he produced a safety lamp for miners, which could be used safely in areas where methane gas had collected.

- In 1821, he was given the job of designing the Stockton and Darlington Railway. It opened in 1825 and used his company's locomotives.

- Designed and made locomotives for the first city-to-city line – Liverpool to Manchester – which opened in 1830.

Supporter: Written by modern historian Bob Fowke, in *Who? What? When? Victorians*

'Before the coming of the railways, the fastest anyone could travel was the speed of a galloping horse. By the time George Stephenson retired, you could travel from London to Newcastle by train in just nine hours, at an average speed of approximately 28 miles per hour. It was Stephenson, the son of a fireman in the Northumberland mines, more than anyone else, who created the British railway system… before he retired in 1845, he had designed most of the railway which connects the major cities of the North of England.'

SOURCE B: *George Stephenson, with images of his most famous train (the* Rocket*) and a bridge over the Stockton and Darlington Railway, appeared on British £5 notes between 1990 and 2003.*

Nominee No. 4: Michael Faraday
Nickname: **The electricity king**

- Born in Newington in 1791, the son of a blacksmith.

- Worked in a bookshop where he became fascinated by science. He taught himself all he knew!

- He was most interested in electricity and magnetism and, in 1831, discovered how to generate electricity.

- His generator worked on the same basic principle that electric power stations work on today. The rim of a copper wheel passes between the poles of a magnet. When the wheel turns, electric current flows in the copper.

- When Faraday died in 1867, it was discovered that he had kept notes on *every* aspect of his research – he always numbered the paragraphs of his notes, the last paragraph being number 3299.

SOURCE C: *The Bank of England thought Faraday was so important it put him on the £20 note from 1991 to 1999.*

Supporter: From the Royal Institution website, an organization devoted to scientific education and research

'… He is one of the world's most important scientists. His discoveries… helped to make the modern world how we know it today. He made discoveries that made… it possible for us all to switch on lights, cook our dinner, play on games consoles. He also invented the electric motor which not only is used in all cars, but is also used in fans, washing machines and hair dryers.'

Nominee No. 5: Charles Babbage
Nickname: **The father of the computer**

- Born in London in 1791.

- Rich parents, excellent education.

- In the early 1800s, a 'computer' was a person who worked out long, complicated maths sums for scientists, engineers and designers. But the 'computers' (i.e. the people) often made mistakes.

- So in the 1820s, Babbage designed several machines to do the calculations, instead of humans.

- Babbage never actually finished one of his calculating machines, but in 1991 (200 years after Babbage's birth), the Science Museum in London decided to build it… and it worked perfectly!

- Babbage also wrote books on code-breaking and designed things to make trains safer.

SOURCE D: *A photograph of Charles Babbage… and his brain! He donated half of his brain to the Science Museum in London, where it is on display.*

Supporter: Adapted from an article on the *Primer Magazine* website (www.primermagazine.com)

'If you use a computer you have Charles Babbage to thank… the original "computers" were actually people who worked out long mathematical equations. In the 1800s, one gentleman invented a machine that did the maths instead of the man… Even though Babbage's machines were mechanical, they have a lot in common with a modern computer – the data and programme memory were separated and operation was instruction based, for example.'

Nominee No. 6: Isambard Kingdom Brunel
Nickname: A master engineer

- Born in Portsmouth in 1806, the son of Marc Brunel, the first man to build a tunnel under the River Thames.

- At 23, he designed the Clifton Suspension Bridge in Bristol. He once worked for 96 hours without a break!

- In 1833, he designed and built the Great Western Railway, said by some to be the best railway ever built. He also built two grand stations – Paddington (London) and Temple Meads (Bristol).

- As a shipbuilder, Brunel designed three record-breaking ships:
  - The *Great Western* – Launched in 1837, steam-powered and the biggest ship in the world. Crossed the Atlantic in a record 15 days.
  - The *Great Britain* – Launched in 1843, the world's first all-iron ship with a screw propeller instead of paddles.
  - The *Great Eastern* – Launched in 1858, again steam-powered and a new 'world's largest ship' record breaker. It carried 4000 passengers and laid the first underwater communications cable between America and Britain.

- In 2002, BBC TV asked people to vote for 'the Greatest Briton'. In the end, Winston Churchill came first… but Brunel came second.

SOURCE A: *Brunel pictured in front of one of the anchor chains of the* Great Eastern, *1858.*

Supporter: Written by the modern historian Susan Willoughby, in *Britain, 1750–1900*

'Britain needed engineers between 1750 and 1900. They designed roads, canals, locks, bridges, railways and tunnels. This was important work. It helped Britain to become a great industrial country. Brunel is a good example of an engineer at this time.'

Nominee No. 7:
Henry Bessemer
Nickname: Man of steel

- Born near Hitchin, Hertfordshire, in 1813.

- Designed a machine for putting perforations on postage stamps and a new method of producing glass.

- In 1856, he was asked by the government to make a cannon that wouldn't shatter under the force of a shell being fired from it.

- He invented a 'converter', a machine for turning iron into steel (see **Source C**). Soon all the pots, furniture, railways and machinery that had been made from iron were made from steel instead. He made 100 per cent profit every other month for 14 years!

- In 1850, Britain produced 60,000 tons of steel – by 1880, 1.25 million tons were produced.

- In America, where his ideas were copied, eight cities and towns are named after him.

SOURCE B: *Sir Henry Bessemer.*

SOURCE C: *The huge container is filled with a white-hot liquid iron. A blast of hot air is blown through the bottom of the container. This removes many of the* **impurities**. *After a few chemicals are added to the swirling hot mass, the container is full of steel. Simple, eh!*

Supporter: Written by Andrew Langley in *Victorian Britain*

'With Henry Bessemer's invention of his converter in 1856, steel could at last be made from iron quickly and cheaply. Steel was stronger and less brittle than iron and many new uses were found for it. Railways were re-laid with steel track. Great steel bridges were built to carry the lines over wide rivers… Steel also brought a great change to shipbuilding. It was lighter than iron, so bigger ships could be made.'

Nominee No. 8: Alexander Graham Bell
Nickname: The king of communication

- Born in Edinburgh, Scotland, in 1847.
- Moved to Canada in 1870, then America a year later.
- Married a deaf woman, and worked all his life on making electrical hearing aids for deaf people.
- The idea for a telephone – a machine that converts speech into an electrical signal that travels down a wire and is then turned back into sound – came to him while working on designs to help deaf people.
- Invented the telephone in 1876. Lots of people were trying to make telephones at this time and Bell was accused of copying some of the designs of other inventors.

Supporter: From an article on Alexander Graham Bell on www.westerncultureglobal.org

'The telephone is arguably the greatest communication device created. It requires no special skill to operate; provides personal, real-time and efficient communication; can reach across the globe in seconds; and can be inexpensive to use… Bell was responsible for numerous other inventions, including the metal detector.'

SOURCE D: *Alexander Graham Bell with sketches of his early designs.*

SOURCE E: *The world's first ever telephone, used by Alexander Graham Bell in 1876.*

Work

1. Imagine you work for the organizers of the special award ceremony. You are writing the programme given to guests as they arrive. Prepare it using this guideline:
   - Plan the programme carefully – A5 or A4 paper?
   - Write clearly – writing drafts first is always best!
   - Give facts, dates and figures about each candidate. What did they invent or design? When? How?
   - Only pack the programme with information; do not give your opinions.
   - Include a front cover, mentioning the name of the award ceremony and the eight contenders.

2. Have a debate: 'Who deserves our National Award for Invention and Design?'
   a. Choose a favourite: Arkwright, Babbage, Bell, Bessemer, Brunel, Faraday, Stephenson or Watt.
   b. Write a persuasive speech about your favourite, trying to convince others that he deserves the award. Use powerful adjectives that will make him seem great, for example, '_____ was amazing because…'. Mention how important his contribution was to the field of invention and design. For example, '_____ was important because…'.
   c. Eight pupils could volunteer to speak, one for each inventor or designer. Each speaker should try to persuade the class to vote for their man. The rest of the class should think of questions to ask each speaker.
   d. After the speeches, hold a class vote, perhaps in secret, to decide who wins.

Today we are surrounded by machines that make our lives easier… or better… or safer! If we decide to visit someone who lives 10km away, we can do it quickly and with very little effort. If we see a beautiful sunset or a famous landmark, we don't have to reach for a set of paints, we grab a camera. To enjoy music, we don't have to actually play an instrument or sing, we can listen to songs recorded by people who are much more talented than us! The period in history that arguably brought the greatest number of new inventions was the nineteenth century… and many of these fabulous ideas are still part of our lives today. Some helped out at home or at work, or improved our health. Others provided a way of communicating on a global scale. Some helped people run businesses and broadcast news. Not all of these inventions were British… but they have had an enormous impact on life in Britain. So what inventions have made the greatest impact on *your* life?

Mission Objectives

- Identify three inventions from the eighteenth and nineteenth centuries that have made a huge impact on your life today.
- Judge which you think is the most important invention and why.

Scottish inventor Robert Thomson makes a pneumatic tyre – a tyre filled with air! **1845**

Chloroform gas first used as an anaesthetic by Scotsman James Simpson **1847**

1849 American mechanic Walter Hunt invents the modern safety pin

1849 American Isaac Singer produces his mechanical sewing machine

Dorset-born William Henry Fox Talbot demonstrates how to develop photographs onto paper **1839**

American Samuel Morse invents 'Morse Code', a system of sending messages over long distances in the form of dots and dashes **1838**

Two British inventors, William Cooke (from Middlesex) and Charles Wheatstone (from Gloucester), invent an 'electric telegraph' – a machine capable of sending messages along wires **1837**

American Jacob Perkins invents the practical refrigerator **1834**

Italian Alessandro Volta invents the first electric battery **1800**

Steam train invented by Cornishman Richard Trevithick **1804**

Peter Durand, from Middlesex, England, invents the tin can **1810**

1831 British scientist Michael Faraday invents the electric motor

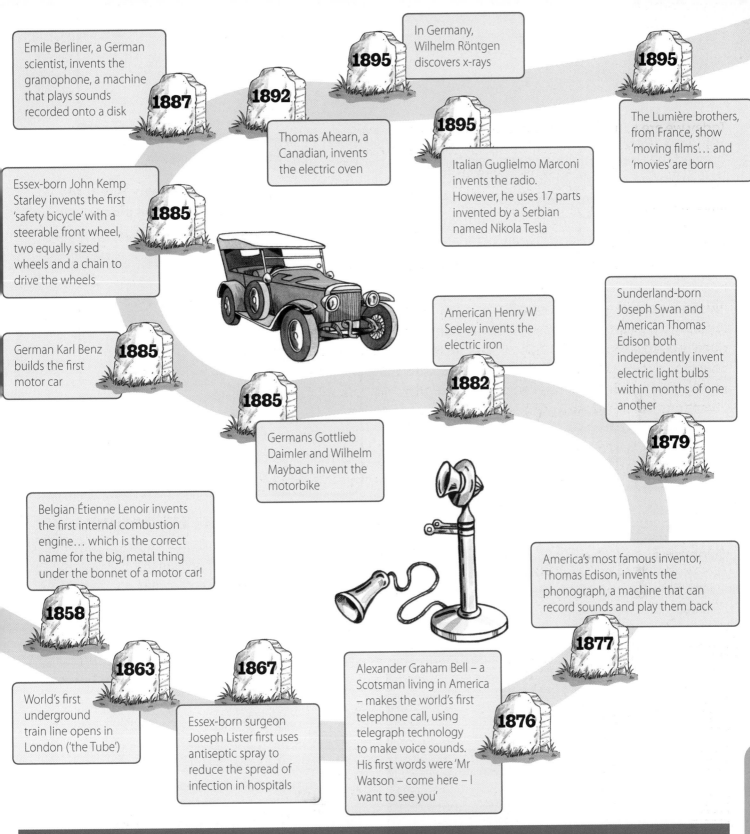

Emile Berliner, a German scientist, invents the gramophone, a machine that plays sounds recorded onto a disk

1887

1892

Thomas Ahearn, a Canadian, invents the electric oven

1895

In Germany, Wilhelm Röntgen discovers x-rays

1895

Italian Guglielmo Marconi invents the radio. However, he uses 17 parts invented by a Serbian named Nikola Tesla

1895

The Lumière brothers, from France, show 'moving films'... and 'movies' are born

Essex-born John Kemp Starley invents the first 'safety bicycle' with a steerable front wheel, two equally sized wheels and a chain to drive the wheels

1885

German Karl Benz builds the first motor car

1885

1885

Germans Gottlieb Daimler and Wilhelm Maybach invent the motorbike

American Henry W Seeley invents the electric iron

1882

Sunderland-born Joseph Swan and American Thomas Edison both independently invent electric light bulbs within months of one another

1879

Belgian Étienne Lenoir invents the first internal combustion engine… which is the correct name for the big, metal thing under the bonnet of a motor car!

1858

1863

World's first underground train line opens in London ('the Tube')

1867

Essex-born surgeon Joseph Lister first uses antiseptic spray to reduce the spread of infection in hospitals

Alexander Graham Bell – a Scotsman living in America – makes the world's first telephone call, using telegraph technology to make voice sounds. His first words were 'Mr Watson – come here – I want to see you'

1876

America's most famous inventor, Thomas Edison, invents the phonograph, a machine that can record sounds and play them back

1877

Work

1 Choose ten inventions from this timeline that have had a direct impact on your life. Explain what this impact has been.

2 **a** Pick five from your list of ten and place the inventions in order of their importance – but write down the five using morse code!

b Write a paragraph explaining why you have put them in the order you have.

3 What invention **not** on the timeline (so it could be a modern one) could you not live without? Explain why.

How great was the Great Exhibition?

On 1 May 1851, Queen Victoria and her husband, Prince Albert, opened the Great Exhibition. It was held in London's Hyde Park in a huge, specially built glass hall. It was the world's first international exhibition and was designed to show the very latest goods you could find in the world. Nothing like this had ever been done before and Queen Victoria was really excited – she visited twice before the exhibition officially opened!

Mission Objectives

- Investigate why the Great Exhibition took place.
- Judge how successful it was.

What could people see?

The exhibition was Prince Albert's idea. He wanted the world to see how fantastic Britain was. Visitors could see over 14,000 exhibits from Britain, its colonies and 39 foreign countries. They could walk through a French section, a Chinese gallery or an Indian room. There were separate areas for modern machines, arts and crafts, and manufactured goods. Items on display included: a full-size steam train; a printing press that printed 100,000 sheets of newspaper in one hour; a massive diamond called the Koh-i-noor; and champagne made from rhubarb.

SOURCE A: *One of the more bizarre exhibits was George Merryweather's invention called the* Tempest Prognosticator. *It predicted storms using live leeches! Kept in bottles, the leeches become agitated when a storm is approaching, and their movements trigger a small hammer, which strikes a warning bell.*

FACT!

The Great Exhibition building was known as the Crystal Palace. It was designed by Joseph Paxton, a gardener famous for building greenhouses.

- It was 563m long and 140m at its widest point.
- 4572 tons of iron framework supported 293,655 panes of glass made in the Midlands.
- It took nine months to build and cost £335,742.

How popular was the exhibition?

- It attracted over six million visitors – around a third of all people in Britain! Trains ran from all over the country so ordinary workers could come.
- Visitors paid 5p for the day (around £4.50 in today's money), and they could buy a huge range of food and drink. A company, Schweppes, provided many of the drinks, and a steam-powered freezer made ice-cream on the spot!
- The exhibition made about £200,000 in profit. Prince Albert wanted to encourage 'useful knowledge' so he spent the money building the Victoria and Albert Museum, the Science Museum, the Natural History Museum and the Royal Albert Hall.

What did people say?

Some protests were made against the building, but many people loved it:

A gust of wind could blow it down and kill everyone inside!

So many people will come into contact with each other that another great plague will hit Britain!

It is a Palace of the People. Our Queen herself called it 'one of the wonders of the world'.

SOURCE B: *An 1854 illustration of the Great Exhibition.*

So where did the building go?

The Great Exhibition closed after six months. Britain had shown the world what a great nation it was and had enjoyed showing off. For the next 20 years, Britain dominated world trade as many countries became desperate to buy British goods.

The building itself was taken to pieces and moved to south-east London. A huge garden was built around it that attracted visitors for many years. A sports ground was built nearby which was used for FA Cup Finals until 1914 (and a football club was formed to use the pitch too – they called themselves Crystal Palace FC!).

Sadly the building was destroyed by fire in 1936. Now, only the gardens remain.

Hungry for More?

Design an exhibition that celebrates the country we live in today. What would the exhibition be like? Write a proposal or plan a presentation that includes a plan or description of the building and the kind of exhibits you would include.

What Happened When?

1851

In the same year as the Great Exhibition, a British explorer (Edward Hargraves) found gold in Australia. This started a 'gold rush' in the country as thousands of people travelled there in search of their fortunes.

Work

1. **a** Why was the Great Exhibition held?
   b What contributions did these people make to the exhibition?
      i Joseph Paxton
      ii Prince Albert
2. In your opinion, do you think the Great Exhibition was a success or not? Give reasons for your answer.

3. Imagine you are a Victorian visitor to the exhibition. Write a letter to a friend about your day.
   - What did you see? Don't just write a list; write what you felt about what you saw.
   - Use lots of powerful verbs and adjectives.
   - Why was the exhibition so popular?

So what was the Industrial Revolution?

Historians like to give labels to different periods of time – the 'Ice Age', the 'Stone Age', the 'Norman Conquest', the 'Middle Ages' and the 'Tudor Period' are all good examples. The period of time covered in this book also has a label. It is often called the **Industrial Revolution**. These two pages aim to discover how it got its name… and what caused this Industrial Revolution to happen.

Mission Objectives

- Explain what is meant by the term 'Industrial Revolution'.
- Analyse and understand the causes of the Industrial Revolution.

All Change!

Huge changes occurred in the way people worked in the 1700s and 1800s. This was the time when the **manufacturing** of goods moved out of people's homes and into the new steam-powered factories. Dozens of clever machines made things in a fraction of the time it would have taken a person. 'Industrial' is another word for 'work' and 'revolution' is another word for 'change'. Certainly then, during this time, industry in Britain had undergone a significant revolution.

Most historians agree that there wasn't just one thing that caused the Industrial Revolution. Instead, there was a combination of several factors that all came together at a similar time.

FACT!

By 1830, one operator working several factory machines could produce 3500 times more cloth than a person working at home could have done in 1700!

More people

Between 1745 and 1901, the population increased – massively.

All these people needed shirts, coats, shoes, plates, clocks and so on. The factories that produced these goods made a fortune for their owners – and there was plenty of work to go around too! Britain changed as factories provided work for the growing population… and made lots of goods for them to buy.

Empire

During this time, Britain gained a vast empire. At one point, Britain ruled about 450 million people living in 56 colonies all over the world. Britain ruled huge countries like Canada, India, Australia – and much of North America, up to 1783. Britain's was the biggest empire the world had ever known! These colonies bought British-made goods of all kinds, especially cloth, iron and, later, steel.

Britain changed as its empire grew. Cheap goods, like cotton, were imported from the colonies; the factories turned it into cloth… and sold some of it back for enormous profits!

Clever entrepreneurs

Entrepreneurs are business people who are prepared to take risks. They buy **raw materials** (like clay), make it into goods (like teapots) and sell the goods for a profit. At this time, there were large numbers of risk-taking entrepreneurs. Banks were willing to lend them money to put into new businesses, factories and inventions if it looked like they would be profitable.

Brilliant inventors

At this time, some of the world's greatest inventors happened to live in Britain. Clever inventors thought up wonderful machines that did things faster than ever before. Steam engines, steam trains, electric generators, telephones and light bulbs are just a few 'British firsts'. Britain changed as it became a world leader in technology.

Coal and iron

Britain was blessed with some valuable raw materials. By 1850, Britain produced two-thirds of the world's coal, half of the world's iron, two-thirds of the world's steel and half of the world's cotton cloth! No wonder Britain was sometimes called the 'workshop of the world'. Others just called it 'Great Britain'.

Wise Up Words

entrepreneur   Industrial Revolution
manufacture   raw material

Be a Top Historian

Top historians know that the big changes, like the Industrial Revolution, have a number of **causes**. Sometimes the causes of an event are linked. This is what task **2** in the Work section challenges you to recognize.

Work

1   In your own words, explain what 'Industrial Revolution' means.

2   All the following factors were important in creating an 'Industrial Revolution' in Britain. Your task is to show how these factors worked together:

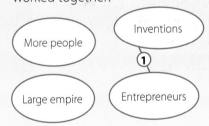

Key: ① *Entrepreneurs were able to take the new inventions and make them into profitable businesses. This created jobs and wealth.*

a   Copy the diagram into your book.
b   Draw lines between the factors that you think are connected in some way.
c   Give each line a number and, below your diagram, explain the connection between the factors.
To help you get started, one connection has been drawn and explained for you.

Assessing Your Learning 1

What can a painting tell us?

Historians use lots of sources. They use them as clues to tell them about the past. A source can be a document or diary (written sources), pictures, paintings, posters, buildings and artefacts (objects), for example. They might help tell us how people lived or what people thought or believed.

Looking at sources can be lots of fun and often involves you thinking hard and making interesting observations and discoveries. Sometimes the source doesn't tell you something directly, you have to 'read between the lines' and try to work out what the person who wrote the source or painted the picture was *really* trying to tell you. This is called **inference** – and finding things out from a source that it doesn't obviously tell you is an important history skill!

Over to you

This is a very famous picture by an artist called William Hogarth. It was drawn in 1751 and is called *Gin Lane*. But Hogarth wasn't actually painting a 'real' scene of something he'd seen, he was exaggerating in order to make a point about how people lived and behaved at this time. He'd certainly seen similar behaviour over the years but was trying to bring it all together in one picture to show the dangers of drinking cheap gin, a drink that was readily available.

Your first task

1. Try to find:

   a. the drunk mother dropping her baby

   b. the dead alcoholic whose dog is sitting next to him

   c. the entrances to two pubs, shown by gin tankards hanging over the doors

   d. the desperate (and poor) man and woman trying to sell their pots and pans to get money for gin. The shop is a pawnbroker's and people would sell their goods during the week and buy them back when they were paid!

   e. gin being fed to a baby

   f. the drunk men playing around in a wheelbarrow

   g. the dead woman being lowered into her coffin – what do you think has caused her death?

   h. the dead man hanging by a rope inside his house – was it suicide perhaps? If so, why might he have killed himself?

   i. the house about to fall on those below – why wasn't money spent on repairing the building?

   j. the man sharing his bone with a dog – is he too poor to eat properly… or is he too drunk to care?

Next step

2. Why do you think Hogarth drew this picture?

3. Do you think it got the message across about the dangers of drinking gin? Explain your answer carefully.

> **TOP TIP:** Sentence starters to help you when writing about 'inference':
> - From [detail from picture], I can infer that…
> - This [detail from picture] suggests to me that… because…

4. Imagine you have been given the job of writing about the drawing for inclusion in a gallery's guidebook. Write a short description of *Gin Lane*. Include facts and figures about the drawing (artist, date, topic) and several features to look out for. You must not use more than 150 words!

> **Hungry for More?**
>
> Find all the babies and children in the picture. What do you think Hogarth wants us to think about what's happening to them?

Assessing your work

For these four tasks, look at the success criteria to help you plan and evaluate your work:

Good	In a **good** response, you would…	• describe a variety of images/scenes within the picture • explain what Hogarth wanted people viewing the picture to think • produce a clear and concise description using simple sentences with the correct dates and historical terms.
Better	In a **better** response, you would…	• identify why Hogarth drew this picture at this time • select different images in the picture and relate this information to Hogarth's key message • structure your work clearly and carefully, using the correct historical terms and dates.
Best	In the **best** response, you would…	• outline why a range of images have been used in the picture to get across Hogarth's message • explain how paintings and pictures can be useful to historians • select, organize and use relevant information to produce a concise, structured description.

What made Sheffield stink?

In 1850, the writer Charles Reade wrote about the town of Sheffield in the north of England. He described it as 'perhaps the most hideous town in creation'. He reported that black smoke blocked out the sun and 'sparkling streams entered the town... but soon got filthy, full of rubbish, clogged with dirt and bubbling with rotten, foul-smelling gasses'. So what made Sheffield stink?

Mission Objective

• Investigate what life was like for thousands of ordinary people in newly expanded industrial towns like Sheffield in the nineteenth century.

A changing nation

Sheffield was no different to many other British towns at this time. Places such as Manchester, Liverpool and Birmingham were equally bad. Why, then, had these towns become such horrible places to live? The answer: once a factory had been built, people would flood in from the countryside to find work. Factory owners then had to build homes for the workers. Houses were built quickly and cheaply, and were crammed close together with narrow alleys between them. Built in **terraces**, the houses were also built **back-to-back** to save space and money.

There was no planning or quality control and some homes were even built without foundations. In 1842, one factory owner went to visit his workers in a row of newly built houses and found that they had all blown down after a storm the night before.

FACT!

Do you have to share a bedroom? Imagine what it would be like to share your bed with up to *seven* others! A survey in 1839 found that out of 3000 families in Bury, 773 of them slept with three or four to a bed; 209 had five in a bed; 67 had six in a bed and, in 15 families, seven people slept in one bed.

SOURCE B: *Back-to-back houses in Liverpool.*

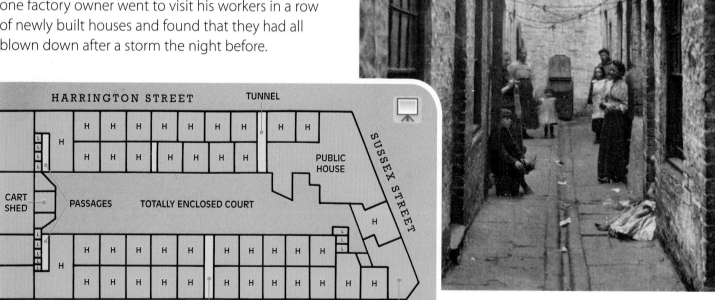

SOURCE A: *A plan of back-to-back housing in Nottingham, 1845.*

H HOUSE   L LAVATORY

A changing Sheffield

The dramatic change in Sheffield is best illustrated by two images. **Source C** is a picture of Sheffield painted in 1738. What words would you use to describe it? What are the important features?

Source D shows Sheffield over 100 years later, in the middle of the nineteenth century. What is different? What now dominates the town?

SOURCE D: *Sheffield in 1884.*

SOURCE C: *Sheffield in 1738.*

Work

1   Look at **Sources C** and **D**. Imagine you had been able to visit Sheffield in 1738 (Source C) and again in 1884 (Source D). Describe the changes that would have made the biggest impression on you.

2   **a**   Look at **Source E**. Draw a bar chart to represent the growth in population of each of the five towns.

   b   In your own words, explain why industrial towns grew so quickly in the 1800s.

3   Look at **Source A**.

   a   Draw the plan of back-to-back houses.

   b   What is missing from these houses that we take for granted today?

   c   On your plan, mark which house (or houses) you would least like to live in. Give reasons for your choice.

Town	Population 1750	Population 1801	Population 1851
Liverpool	35,000	82,000	376,000
Birmingham	30,000	71,000	233,000
Leeds	14,000	53,000	172,000
Manchester	45,000	75,000	303,000
Sheffield	20,000	46,000	135,000

SOURCE E: *In 1801, only eight towns in England, Wales and Scotland had more than 50,000 people living there: Birmingham, Bristol, Edinburgh, Glasgow, Leeds, Liverpool, London and Manchester. By 1900, there were over 60.*

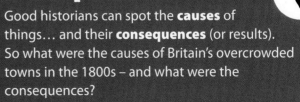

Be a Top Historian

Good historians can spot the **causes** of things… and their **consequences** (or results). So what were the causes of Britain's overcrowded towns in the 1800s – and what were the consequences?

Overcrowding

Almost all the houses in the largest towns across Britain were crowded; usually with five or more people living in one small room, which they rented from a local landlord or the factory owners themselves. In 1847, 40 people were found sharing one room in Liverpool!

Sewage

The disposal of sewage was a major problem. None of the houses had toilets indoors, so the best some families could manage was a bucket in the corner of the room. This would be emptied now and again, either into the street or stored outside the door until there was enough to sell to a farmer as manure. Occasionally, there was a street toilet (a deep hole with a wooden shed over it) but this would have to be shared with 30 or 40 other families. Sometimes a pump provided water but often the water came from the local river… and this would be filthy. There were no rubbish collections, litter bins, street cleaners, sewers or fresh running water.

'There is a huge dunghill here. The owner sells it. He gets more money for older dung. The pile smells so badly that people nearby have to keep their food covered because it tastes of the dunghill!'

SOURCE A: *A doctor describes a street in Scotland for a government report in 1842.*

Medical problems

Sewage trickled down the streets and into nearby rivers. Yet, most families washed themselves in and drank from the same river. It was little wonder that disease thrived in towns. In 1840, one in every three children died before they reached five. In Leeds, the average age of death for a working-class man was 19 and in Manchester it was 17.

KEY FOR SOURCE B:

A Drinking in pubs was a favourite pastime. People mostly drank beer but gin was also common.

B A dunghill.

C Night soilmen taking away sewage to sell.

D Crime was common and there was no national police force until the 1850s.

E A shared street toilet.

F A water pump, which often pulled up water from the river.

G People used the river to wash their clothes and collect drinking water.

H Water carriers sold water in the streets (but some just got water from the river).

I Rats, a common sight in nineteenth-century towns.

J Families living in one room.

K This family is sick. **Cholera** was the new killer disease – those who caught it turned black and blue, got violently sick and had terrible diarrhoea. About half of those who got it died within 24 hours. In some areas, the cemeteries had to be closed because they were too full.

L 'Costermongers' hired carts, bought food from local markets and wandered the streets selling door-to-door.

M A factory.

N The houses were in a poor state of repair. Landlords cared little about the state of the houses – and there were no laws to make sure they looked after their properties.

Work

1 a Make a list of factors about life in towns that might lead to poor health and disease.
   b Make another list of ways the government could improve living conditions.

2 Look at **Source A**.
   a What is 'dung'?
   b What did the dunghill owner do with his dung?
   c Who might have wanted to buy dung and why?
   d How did the dunghill affect people in the neighbourhood?

3 Imagine you were unlucky enough to spend a day looking around the streets and visiting houses such as the one featured in **Source B**. Write a letter home to a friend describing what you have seen.
   • Can you explain why industrial towns like Sheffield expanded so quickly in the nineteenth century?
   • Can you explain what problems this expansion brought with it?
   Make sure your letter is set out correctly; with an address, date, greeting, and sign-off.

Welcome to Sickness Street

Disease thrived in towns. In 1840, one in every five children died before their first birthday and one in three died before they reached five. In Manchester, the average age of death for an ordinary working man was 17. Astonishing! People had been attracted to towns by the promise of jobs in factories. But the reality of living in the **squalor** of these ever-expanding towns was the damaging effect it had on people's health. So what did people die of in these places?

Mission Objectives

- Identify four of the most common diseases in the nineteenth century.
- Propose why disease was so common at the time.

SOURCE A: *A photograph of back-to-back houses in Liverpool.*

Smallpox

- **How?** Germs are passed from one person to another by coughing, sneezing or in some cases touching.

- **Symptoms?** A rash turns into huge pus-filled blisters all over the body. When the blisters drop off, they leave deep scars. It can kill.

- **Who?** Can attack and kill people of all ages. Killed up to 60 per cent of adults and 80 per cent of children infected.

Cholera

- **How?** Caused by a germ that lives in contaminated water. If you caught cholera, there was a 9 out of 10 chance you would die.

- **Symptoms?** 'Cholera' is the Greek word for diarrhoea. As the diarrhoea became worse, victims could keep no food or water in their bodies. They would **dehydrate** and die – sometimes within 24 hours.

- **Who?** Can attack anyone. In Britain, 32,000 people died from cholera in 1831, 62,000 in 1848, 20,000 in 1854 and 14,000 in 1866. These were known as **epidemics**.

Typhoid

- **How?** The typhoid germ lives in urine and poo! Sometimes this **contaminated** water or food. Urgh! This killer disease can also be carried by flies, which land on food.

- **Symptoms?** Headaches, fever, **constipation**… then terrible diarrhoea. A similar disease called typhus was common too, caused by bites from body lice.

- **Who?** Can attack anyone, killed up to 40 per cent of people who got it.

Tuberculosis (TB)

- **How?** Germs are passed from one person to another in the moisture sprayed when people cough or sneeze. Sometimes called 'consumption'. Another type of TB was caused by infected cows' milk. Why do you think this infected more children than adults?

- **Symptoms?** Attacked the lungs. A victim would cough up blood, lose weight, get a fever, chest pains and shortness of breath. It can kill.

- **Who?** Can attack anyone. Infected one out of ten people in the nineteenth century. In 1800, TB was the cause of one in four deaths in London.

SOURCE B: *A poem from* Punch *magazine, 1849.*

THE WATER THAT JOHN DRINKS.

THIS is the water that JOHN drinks.

This is the Thames with its cento of stink,
That supplies the water that JOHN drinks.

These are the fish that float in the ink-
-y stream of the Thames with its cento of stink,
That supplies the water that JOHN drinks.

This is the sewer, from cesspool and sink,
That feeds the fish that float in the ink-
-y stream of the Thames with its cento of stink,
That supplies the water that JOHN drinks.

These are vested int'rests, that fill to the brink,
The network of sewers from cesspool and sink,
That feed the fish that float in the ink-
-y stream of the Thames, with its cento of stink,
That supplies the water that JOHN drinks.

This is the price that we pay to wink
At the vested int'rests that fill to the brink,
The network of sewers from cesspool and sink,
That feed the fish that float in the ink-
-y stream of the Thames with its cento of stink,
That supplies the water that JOHN drinks.

Wise Up Words

constipation   contaminate
dehydrate   epidemic   squalor

Death in the streets

In filthy overcrowded places like Leeds and Manchester, diseases spread very quickly. The average age of death for a working-class man in Leeds was 19! But, unlike today, ordinary people in the towns didn't know that germs could cause disease. Far away in laboratories, some doctors had started to make the connection, but down in the streets and slums of Britain, people continued to live their lives and get their filthy water in the same way that they had always done. It would be many years before the health problems caused by the rapid growth of the towns were tackled.

FACT!

Were the rich as likely to die as the poor? In December 1861, Prince Albert, husband of Queen Victoria, caught typhoid and died. He was 42. The filthy water from one of his palace toilets had leaked into his drinking water.

Work

1 Write a sentence or two to explain these words:
- squalor
- contaminate
- epidemic.

2 Using the facts on page 58, copy these headings in your book and complete the information for each killer disease.
- Name of killer disease
- How did people catch it?
- What happened when they got it?
- Why was it so common?

TOP TIP: Think about how living conditions made it more likely to catch a disease.

3 Look at **Source B**.
a In your own words, sum up what is being said about 'John' in the poem.
b What point do you think the writer of this poem was trying to make?
c Try to write your own version of this poem based on what you've learned about living conditions and disease so far.

4 a How did Prince Albert die?
b Does his death surprise you? Give a reason for your answer.

Who were the heroes of public health?

Ordinary men, women and children (like us) are sometimes called the 'public'. So the state of ordinary people's health and well-being is sometimes known as 'public health'. And in the early 1800s, public health in Britain was in a very poor state. The national average age of death for a working British man, for example, was 30 – that's right, just 30 years of age! In some places, like Liverpool, it was 15! So that meant that in Liverpool you would generally live for just 15 years before you died. So why were things so bad? Why were people dying so young? And what was eventually done – and by whom – to improve the state of the nation's health?

Stinking cities

Towns and cities grew really quickly in the 1800s. Manchester's population, for example, grew from 45,000 in 1745 to over 300,000 by 1851. And the faster towns grew, the worse living conditions became. New housing was built very quickly, very badly and wherever there was space. Lots of families shared these houses, yet they lacked basics such as toilets and running water. And with no one to clean these towns and no sewers to take away the waste, rubbish and sewage piled up in the streets and floated in the rivers. The smell was terrible.

Deadly disease

In these filthy, overcrowded conditions, disease and sickness spread very quickly – but by far the most feared illness was a new one called **cholera**. It first arrived in Britain in 1831 and killed thousands within a year. Victims were violently sick and suffered from painful diarrhoea. Their skin and nails turned black just before the victims fell into a coma and died (see **Source A**). It spread rapidly and people died quickly… and there was no known cure! Some cemeteries became so full that they had to close (see **Source B**).

FACT!

Children's deaths were so common in some towns that the cemeteries had to close. One historian writing about Bilston, West Midlands, said that 'the coffins could not be made fast enough for the dead'.

SOURCE A: *A cholera victim from Sunderland.*

CHOLERA

THE

DUDLEY BOARD OF HEALTH,

HEREBY GIVES NOTICE, THAT IN CONSEQUENCE OF THE

Church-yards at Dudley

Being so full, no one who has died of the CHOLERA will be permitted to be buried after SUNDAY next, (To-morrow) in either of the Burial Grounds of St Thomas's, or St Edmund's, in this Town.

All persons who die from CHOLERA, must for the future be buried in the Church-yard at Netherton.

BOARD OF HEALTH, DUDLEY

SOURCE B: *A copy of a cholera notice in Dudley, West Midlands.*

Did the government do anything?

Special groups – called **Boards of Health** – were set up by some towns to investigate the cholera outbreaks, but they didn't do much, mainly because they didn't know what was causing it. This was a time, remember, when people didn't know that germs caused disease! And the politicians in London didn't do a great deal either, because many felt it wasn't their job to tell people how to live their lives or ask factory owners and businessmen to build better housing and facilities.

Action... at last!

But cholera kept coming back. After further outbreaks killed thousands more people, the government set up an enquiry to try to find out what was going on in Britain's towns and cities. The man in charge was named Edwin Chadwick and he sent out inspection teams of doctors all over Britain. What he found out is summed up in **Source C**.

What Happened When?

1831

In 1831, the same year as the cholera outbreak in Britain, Charles Darwin set off on his voyage aboard the HMS *Beagle*.

Bad air is caused by rotting dead animals and vegetables, filthy houses and dirty streets.

Disease is caused by bad air.

Medical officers should be appointed in towns to take charge of clearing up.

Deaths happen where there is polluted water.

Sewers and drains must be improved so rubbish and filth are taken away from the cities rather than left to rot.

SOURCE C: *Edwin Chadwick, and conclusions from his report.*

Work

1 a What is meant by the term 'public health'?

 b In your own words, explain the state of public health in Britain in the early 1800s.

2 a Who was Edwin Chadwick?

 b What was wrong with Chadwick's idea about the cause of disease?

The impact of Chadwick's report

Chadwick's report about the filthy state of Britain's towns and cities shocked people. Finally, in 1848 the government passed a new law – the Public Health Act – allowing councils to spend money cleaning up if they wanted to. Some cities, like Liverpool (see **Source A**), made huge improvements, but others didn't bother to do anything… so the filth continued!

Cholera comes back!

However, despite the clean up efforts, cholera and other outbreaks of disease kept happening. In 1848, 62,000 people were killed by cholera, followed by 20,000 in 1854. And it was during the 1854 outbreak that a doctor called John Snow decided to work out – once and for all – what on earth was causing cholera. Now read his amazing story in **Source B**.

LIVERPOOL HEALTH COMMITTEE, 1849

We undertake to do the following:

- Improve toilets in the city
- Remove the piles of human waste
- Close down factories that pollute areas near homes
- Supply clean water
- Widen the streets.

Liverpool Council, 1849

SOURCE A: *Liverpool Council worked hard to clean up its city, but other councils did nothing.*

SOURCE B: *The story of John Snow.*

1 John Snow, born into a poor family in York in 1813, had seen the devastating effects of cholera first hand.

When Snow was training to be a doctor in Newcastle in 1831, a cholera outbreak killed over 300 people.

NEWCASTLE CEMETERY

2 Twenty years later, Snow was working in London as a very successful doctor.

He even treated Queen Victoria when she was pregnant.

3 At this time there were two main theories about how people caught diseases, including cholera.

THEORY 1: The miasma theory

Disease is caused by dirty air, known as 'miasma'. Cholera, for example, is carried through the air like a poisonous gas or an infected mist. The stinking, dirty air coming from the filthy towns causes disease!

THEORY 2: The contagion theory

Disease isn't caused by foul air at all. It's caused by having personal contact with a sick person, their clothes or bedding, for example. The sick person is 'contagious' and passes on the disease to someone else!

4 Snow was a 'contagionist'. In other words, he believed that diseases like cholera were passed on by having some sort of contact with a cholera victim.

'For centuries people have thought that disease was carried around in a poisonous cloud… but not me!'

In 1854, Snow got a chance to try out his theory!

SOURCE C: *How the different classes in a typical town might be divided. Why do you think the richer people built their houses where they did?*

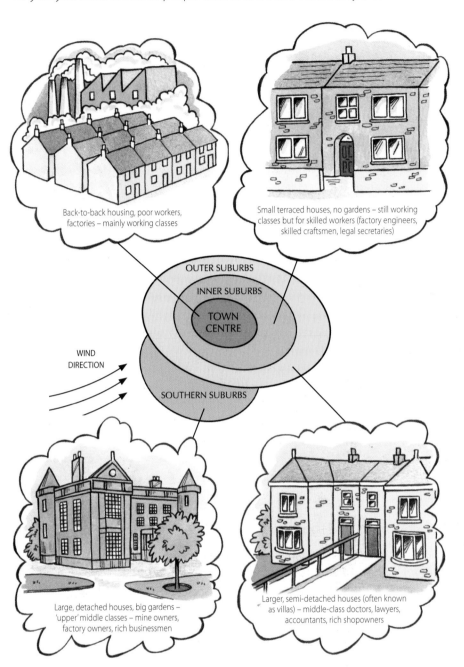

Back-to-back housing, poor workers, factories – mainly working classes

Small terraced houses, no gardens – still working classes but for skilled workers (factory engineers, skilled craftsmen, legal secretaries)

OUTER SUBURBS
INNER SUBURBS
TOWN CENTRE
SOUTHERN SUBURBS

WIND DIRECTION

Large, detached houses, big gardens – 'upper' middle classes – mine owners, factory owners, rich businessmen

Larger, semi-detached houses (often known as villas) – middle-class doctors, lawyers, accountants, rich shopowners

Where did people live?

Your class often determined the part of the town you lived in. The poorer people lived in the centre of town (near the factories) whilst the better off, middle classes lived further out. These 'posher' areas were known as the 'suburbs' (see **Source C**). **Source D** shows how a person's diet might differ too!

Be a Top Historian

It is important that top historians understand that people's lives can be very **different** even if they live in the **same** country in the same period of history.

Wise Up Words

social pyramid

FAMILY 1

Breakfast: Porridge, fried bacon, toast, butter, treacle, marmalade, tea and coffee

Dinner: Boiled mutton (sheep), carrots, turnips, potatoes, bread sauce, jam roly-poly pudding and rice pudding

Tea: Bread, teacakes, butter, cake and tea

Supper: Fish, bread, butter, cake, biscuits, cocoa and oranges

FAMILY 2

Breakfast: Bacon, bread and tea

Dinner: Bacon, bread and tea

Tea: Bacon, bread and tea

Supper: Nothing

SOURCE D: *In 1899, Seebohm Rowntree (his family made chocolate) interviewed two families in York. He asked them what they ate on Monday. No prizes for guessing which family was rich and which was poor.*

Work

1 In your own words, explain what is meant by the word 'class'.

2 Describe the 'social pyramid'.

3 **The Big Write!**

Study all the sources and information on these pages. Imagine that you have been invited to spend a day with an upper-class family and a day with a poorer family. You are a researcher living in the 1800s. Write a diary entry for both days, describing your experiences and feelings about your visits. You should also mention the place where you are staying, the food you eat, the area of town you live in and the way each family spends their time.

Crime and punishment is big news. The latest crime figures, the nastiest murder trials and the state of our prisons are always on our TV screens, on the radio and in newspapers. There are special programmes on TV about catching criminals, and viewing figures for the most popular soap operas go up when a character commits a crime or goes on trial in court.

Mission Objectives

- Identify whose role it was to catch criminals in 1800.
- Explain the terms 'capital crime' and 'transportation'.

Crime and punishment

As a result of all the information about crime and punishment we get from the media, we know a lot about law and order in today's world. But what about a few hundred years ago? How were criminals caught – and who caught them? And how tough were the punishments back then?

Crime was a huge problem in the early 1800s – and life must have been quite easy for Britain's criminals. Many were never caught, for a start, because there were no policemen or detectives to track them down. That's right – there was no police force in the early 1800s, and there never had been! Instead, catching criminals was down to a mixture of people called **magistrates**, **constables** and **watchmen**:

Getting caught

If, by some slim chance, a criminal was caught, the punishments were very tough. This was to act as a warning to others. And the punishments were just as harsh no matter how young the criminal was. In 1801, a boy was executed for breaking into a house and stealing a silver spoon… he was 13 years old! In fact, at this time there were over 200 crimes for which a guilty person could be executed. These were known as **capital crimes** (see **Source A**).

SOME CAPITAL CRIMES

- Murder, treason and arson
- Theft of anything worth more than 25p (around £30 in today's money)
- Stealing from a shipwreck
- Cutting down growing trees
- Being a pirate
- Shooting a rabbit
- Stealing letters
- Blackening up your face at night
- Damaging Westminster Bridge
- Begging without a licence

PLUS ABOUT 180 OTHER CRIMES.

YOU HAVE BEEN WARNED!

▲ **SOURCE A:** *Capital crimes, punishable by death.*

Watchmen

The bigger towns had watchmen (known as Charleys) who patrolled the streets at night. They *were* paid (very badly) and were often too old, fat and feeble to get any other type of job!

Magistrates

Each area had a magistrate. Their job was to question suspects and witnesses in a court. They were unpaid and could punish criminals however they wanted.

Constables

Some areas had one or two constables to help out the magistrates by trying to catch criminals. They were unpaid and did the job for a year before someone else took over.

Harsh punishments

The most common type of execution was hanging… and the public enjoyed watching them. In fact, a public hanging was a day out for all the family and huge crowds turned up to watch. Some rich people rented houses overlooking the **gallows**, and seats in specially built grandstands fetched high prices (see **Source C**). Yet despite the popularity of these hangings, fewer people were hanged than should have been. Courts often took pity on young children or desperate people… even if they had clearly committed a capital crime!

Another common punishment was **transportation** by ship to another place that Britain controlled, like Australia or Gibraltar. Once there, the prisoner became a slave for either five, seven or fourteen years. After this time, they were free to return to Britain, but many never did and settled for a new life abroad. Today, many Australians can trace their ancestors back to criminals transported there in the 1800s.

'The guilty men are placed on a cart, each with a rope around his neck. The cart was driven off under the gallows. Then the criminals' friends come and pull them down by the feet so that they might die all the sooner.'

▲ **SOURCE B:** *Guilty criminals had been killed by public hanging for hundreds of years. Here, a traveller describes an execution.*

SOURCE C: *An execution at Tyburn, London (where Marble Arch stands today).*

Work

1 a Match the words in **List A** with the correct description from **List B**.

List A	List B
Magistrate	Helped the magistrate look after law and order
Constable	Part of a group that watched over the town
Watchman	Questioned suspects in court and gave punishments

  b Think carefully. Why do you think i) magistrates, ii) constables and iii) watchmen were so unreliable?

2 a Explain what is meant by a 'capital crime'. Give three examples.

  b Why were so many people sentenced to death in the early 1800s?

c Why were fewer people executed than should have been?

3 Look at **Source C**. Write down the numbers and beside each one explain what you can see.

4 Read **Source B**.

  a In your own words, explain how the criminal was hanged.

  b Why do you think some of the criminals' friends pulled down on their feet?

5 a Make a list of all the TV shows and soap opera storylines involving crimes and court cases.

  b Why do you think these are so popular?

London had the worst crime problems because it was Britain's largest city. Naturally, it was the place where any crime-fighting initiative would start. In 1749, a London magistrate named Henry Fielding decided to do something about the con men, thieves and prostitutes lurking around his offices in Bow Street. He gathered six men, gave them handcuffs, a pistol and a stick and promised to pay them a guinea (£1.05) a week to capture as many criminals as possible. At first, they wore their own clothes, but were later given a uniform. This force of thief takers became known as the **Bow Street Runners**.

Mission Objectives

- Explain the difference between a Bow Street Runner and one of Peel's 'Bobbies'.
- Assess why Robert Peel established Britain's first police force.

The Bow Street Runners

In 1763, Henry's blind brother, John, set up a horse patrol to stop robbers on the roads in London. By 1792, seven other areas in London had their own versions of the Bow Street Runners. However, as crime levels kept rising, it was clear that the country needed far more. It needed a proper police force!

A new police force

The man who played a major part in creating Britain's first professional police force was an MP named Robert Peel. As the government's Home Secretary, he was responsible for law and order. In 1829, he set up the **Metropolitan Police**. Three thousand men, mainly ex-soldiers, were given a new blue uniform, boots, a wooden truncheon, a rattle, a brown coat and a top hat lined with iron. They received 5p a day (not much then, but better than many other jobs) and were expected to walk their 32km 'beat' around London, seven days a week. They had to be less than 35 years of age, healthy, and able to read and write. Discipline was severe and many early recruits were sacked for drunkenness. London, with its open sewers and filthy air, was so unhealthy that many policemen became poorly.

Call the police!

To begin with, many hated the new police force. Some felt they were a waste of money or spies for the government. Policemen were regularly beaten up in the street and spat at. They were branded 'Peel's bloody gang' and the 'evil blue devils'. But the 'blue devils' did a good job. They were well disciplined, good humoured and acted with restraint wherever possible (see **Source C**). Gradually, the public began to respect and trust them. More criminals were caught, so there was less crime in London too! Soon other towns copied London and, by 1856, every large town had its own policemen.

SOURCE A: *A Bow Street Runner, 1749.*

Labels: Stick, Gun, Handcuffs

SOURCE B: *A policeman, 1829. These men soon became known as 'Peelers' or 'Bobbies' after the surname or Christian name of their founder.*

Labels: Steel-rimmed hat, Handcuffs, Truncheon, Rattle

'You must be polite and attentive to everyone. Rudeness will not be tolerated. You must act quickly and sensibly and have a perfect temper, never allowing yourself to be moved by any foul language or threats... police constables are asked not to pay any attention to any silly expressions which they may be called.'

SOURCE C: *Instructions given to policemen in 1829.*

Catching criminals

In 1810, the old system of the watchmen and the constables brought 9000 convictions. In 1830, there were 18,000 convictions for major crimes. By 1901, there were 48,000 policemen and 25,000 convictions. The new police force seemed to be getting results.

Wise Up Words

Bow Street Runners
Metropolitan Police

SOURCE D: *A photograph of some of Britain's first 'boys in blue', around 1850.*

FACT!

Policemen worked shifts seven days a week. Meal breaks didn't exist, so food was carried in a special blue bag and eaten 'on the beat'. Non-uniformed detectives, based at Scotland Yard, appeared in 1842 (after regular policemen messed up a murder hunt!) but policewomen didn't appear until the twentieth century.

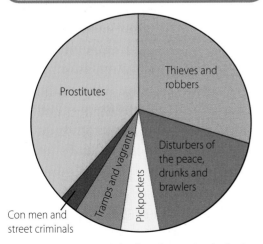

SOURCE E: *London's police record of crimes and criminals, 1837.*

Work

1 Copy out a timeline like the one below.

1740 1750 1760 1770 1780 1790 1800 1810 1820 1830 1840 1850 1860 1870 1880 1890 1900

On the timeline, write in the key events in the history of the Bow Street Runners and the early police forces.

2 a Explain why Robert Peel set up Britain's first police force.
  b Why were some people against the police at first?

3 a Copy the picture of the 1829 policeman (**Source B**). Label your picture clearly.
  b Why do you think he:
    i carried a truncheon?
    ii carried a rattle?
    iii wore a top hat lined with iron?

4 Imagine you are looking for a job in 1829 and you see an advertisement asking for new policemen. Using your knowledge of the type of person Peel was looking for, write a letter to apply, using a formal letter format, and say:
  • Why you want the job
  • What qualities you possess
  • Why Peel should pick you.

4.7 Off to prison

In the early 1800s, a visit to a prison would have been a very harrowing (and smelly) experience. Due to the lack of proper water supply or sewage systems, visitors used handkerchiefs soaked in vinegar or nose clips so they couldn't smell the prisoners. About a quarter of prisoners died each year from disease, and typhus (a virus spread by mice, lice and fleas) was so common it was nicknamed 'jail fever'.

Mission Objectives

- Outline how, and why, prison life changed in the 1800s.
- Assess the significance of Howard and Fry in these changes.

The following story is based on the experiences of Charles Sheppard, a 14-year-old boy. In 1805 he was kept in Shepton Mallet prison in Somerset awaiting trial on a charge of 'stealing a parcel containing five or six knives'.

FACT!

About 60 per cent of inmates were in jail because they owed money – and because they couldn't get out until they'd paid their debts, many stayed in there until they died.

1

I am cold, dirty and starting to feel ill. My cell is filthy and crowded – and we haven't got enough light, water or proper food.

We get porridge and bread every day but it's never enough. And the water we get is so dirty it makes us feel sick to taste it.

2

We don't get provided with beds either but we can hire them from the jailer at 6p per night. I can't afford one so I sleep on the floor on two old rugs that were left over when another prisoner died. I share my bed with the rats, lice and fleas.

3

Prison life is tough. We are forced to work on pointless tasks all day long. We pace the treadmill, a sort of large wheel that goes nowhere; we call it the 'everlasting staircase'. Sometimes we have to unpick old ropes and turn them into doormats – I hate this most of all because it makes my fingers bleed.

4

The jailers who run this place don't get paid – they make their money selling us food, beer, tobacco and blankets. Those who can afford it eat and drink well – the rest of us live on local charity!

5

We get charged for everything in here. There are fees for admission (that's right, we have to pay to get into jail), for release, for food, to have your leg irons removed for a few hours... they're endless!

6

And the most annoying thing of all is that if you're found innocent you can't be released until you pay the money you owe – madness! There are some men who have been in here for decades.

Prison heroes

A man called John Howard was so shocked by the conditions in the prisons that he wrote a best-selling book called *The State of Prisons in England and Wales*. One woman went further than that. After being appalled by what she saw on a visit to Newgate Prison in 1813, Elizabeth Fry spent the rest of her life trying to help the prisoners. She even went into prisons to read Bible stories to the inmates, taught them to read and write, and helped them tidy up their cells (see **Source B**).

Soon, the government began to take notice of Elizabeth Fry and John Howard. Prisons began to change. They still remained tough places to be, but conditions improved. By 1900, official government figures showed that milder treatment led to fewer men returning to prison after they were released.

1820	Whipping of women ended.
1823	Jailers paid wages (so prisoners were not charged for everything). Women prisoners kept separate from the men. Prison doctors, priests and teachers employed. Attempts must be made to reform the prisoners – like teaching them to read and write.
1835	Prison inspectors appointed.
1878	Government takes control of all the prisons. Before this time, nearly half of all prisons were privately owned, with their owners (and their jailers) trying to make as much money as possible out of the prisoners.

▲ **SOURCE A:** *Key dates of prison reforms (1820–1878).*

SOURCE B: *Fry's work was so well respected that, in 2002, she was chosen by the Bank of England to go on its new £5 note.*

Work

1 **a** Why did some visitors to prisons wear nose clips or cover their faces with handkerchiefs soaked in vinegar?

  b Why was disease so common among prisoners?

  c Why did jailers charge prisoners for the things they wanted?

2 **a** How did the following people contribute to the improvement of prison life:
  i John Howard?
  ii Elizabeth Fry?

  b How had prisons improved by 1901? Give examples to support your answer.

3 **The Big Write!**

  Charles Sheppard spent 13 weeks in jail waiting for his trial. When the time came, his accuser failed to turn up at the courthouse – and Charles walked free. Choose any three days in Charles' 13-week stay in jail. Write a diary entry for each of the three days, including details of his experiences and how he felt.

4 What do you think is meant by the sentence, 'The country seemed to be getting more civilized'? Explain your answer carefully. You may want to discuss it as a class first.

What Happened When? `1878`

In 1878, the same year that prison inspectors were appointed in Britain, Thomas Edison patented his phonograph, a machine that can record sounds and play them back.

4.8A What did Jack the Ripper look like?

On 31 August 1888, a London prostitute called Mary Ann Nichols was found murdered. Her throat had been slashed and her stomach cut open with a long-bladed knife. Then, just over a week later, another prostitute called 'Dark Annie' Chapman was found dead not far from the first murder. She'd also been killed with a long-bladed knife and cut open. Some of her internal organs were missing too! And more murders followed, victims of a killer whose nickname is still known around the world today – 'Jack the Ripper'!

So how did the murderer get the nickname 'Jack the Ripper'? How many women did he kill? How did the police try to track him down? Was he ever caught? And what does the Jack the Ripper story tell us about life in Victorian London?

The killer gets a nickname

It didn't take the police long to realize they had a violent serial killer on their hands. Then, on 27 September, a London newspaper received an amazing letter (see **Source B**). The writer boasted of the killings and teased the police for not catching him. Within days, gruesome details of the murders appeared in newspapers all over Britain. The press didn't care whether the letter was from the genuine killer or not, they just knew that descriptions of crimes sold newspapers – and they were happy to print all the details they could. They even began using the name that the writer of the first letter had given himself – Jack the Ripper!

Dear Boss,

I keep on hearing the police have caught me but they haven't. I have laughed when they look so clever and talk about being on the right track. I am down on whores and I shan't quit until I get caught. The last job was good work. I gave the lady no time to squeal. How can they catch me now? I love my work and want to start again. You'll soon hear of me. I saved some of the red stuff in a ginger beer bottle so I could write to you with it, but it went thick like glue and I can't use it. Red ink is fit enough I hope, ha, ha. The next job I shall cut the lady's ears off and send them to the police for fun. My knife's so sharp I want to get to work right away if I get a chance. Good luck.

Yours truly,
Jack the Ripper
Don't mind me giving the nickname
PS They say I'm a doctor now, ha, ha!

▲ **SOURCE B:** *Adapted from 'Jack's' letter, 27 September 1888. Why do you think the police thought 'Jack' was a doctor or a butcher? What do you think the 'red stuff' was that he was writing about? What was 'Jack' intending to do with the 'red stuff'?*

FACT!

As there was no 'dole' money for women without work, many were forced to become prostitutes to survive. Many became alcoholics to escape their terrible lives. It was these women who were the Ripper's prey.

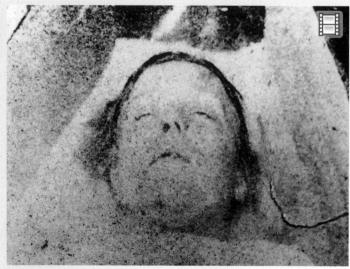

SOURCE A: *A photograph of the corpse of Mary Ann Nichols.*

More murders

On 30 September, two more prostitutes were found murdered. 'Long Liz' Stride and Catherine 'Katie' Eddowes were killed within minutes of each other. Bits of Catherine's blood-soaked clothing were nearby. Later, doctors found that one of her ears, her nose and one of her kidneys had been removed.

More letters

On the morning of 1 October, the same newspaper received another letter (see **Source D**). The letter refers to the 'Double' killing the night before. Expert analysts thought the same person wrote both of the letters that the newspaper had received – but had no way of knowing if they had been written by the real killer or not!

> I wasn't kidding dear old Boss when I gave you the tip. You'll hear about Saucy Jacky's work tomorrow. Double event this time. Number one squealed a bit – couldn't finish straight off. Ha, not the time to get the ears off for police.
>
> Jack the Ripper

▲ **SOURCE D:** *The second letter. Is there any part of this second letter that leads you to think that it might have been written by the same person as the first letter? Is there anything about the words or phrases used that are similar in both letters?*

Then, on 16 October, the police received another letter (**Source E**). The envelope contained a note and a piece of human kidney! Police were unable to tell if the letter came from the same person as the first two letters. However, most detectives felt that different people wrote them.

> From Hell
>
> Sir,
> I send half the kidney I took from one of the women. I cooked and ate the other half. It was very nice. I might send you the knife.
> Catch me if you can

▲ **SOURCE E:** *Letter sent to the police, 16 October 1888. It is known as the 'From Hell' letter. Do you think the third letter is from the same writer as the first two letters? What similarities or differences are there to the first two letters?*

SOURCE C: *An illustration that appeared in a London newspaper in 1888 showing the police discovery of the body of Catherine Eddowes.*

Murder number five

On 9 November, a fifth prostitute (Mary Kelly) was murdered. She was the only Ripper victim to be found indoors. Police found Mary's clothes folded neatly on a chair and her books in front of the fire. She had been cut open, her organs placed around the room and her face hacked to pieces.

SOURCE F: *Mary Kelly's lodging house at 13 Miller's Court the day after her murder. She was seen through the broken window by Thomas Bowyer.*

By mid-November news of the killings had spread all over the world. Stories appeared in 160 newspapers as far away as Australia and Mexico. Even Queen Victoria took a keen interest and urged the police to catch the killer quickly.

4.8B What did Jack the Ripper look like?

How many were killed?

This is unclear. It is generally accepted that he killed five – Nichols, Chapman, Stride, Eddowes and Kelly – but some experts think he killed more. The public, newspapers and some policemen at the time thought he might be responsible for as many as 13 deaths. However, the detectives in charge of the case decided to keep the figure at five.

What was London like in 1888?

London, in 1888, was a divided city. The West End of the city was home to wealthier Londoners while the East End was crowded with the slum housing of the poor. Jack the Ripper operated in the East End, in the so-called 'evil square mile', which included the districts of Whitechapel, Spitalfields and Aldgate. In fact, the East End was the ideal environment for crime. Smoke and stinking gases from factories and housing choked the narrow city streets so badly that, at times, it wasn't possible to see more than a metre in front of your face. Dark passages and alleyways provided excellent cover for any thief, mugger… or murderer.

What did the police do?

The police interviewed over 2000 people, including witnesses who claimed they had seen the victims with 'mysterious-looking' men before their deaths. The police talked to sailors, butchers, doctors and drug addicts. They handed out 80,000 leaflets appealing for information and specially trained sniffer dogs were recruited to 'sniff out' any leads. Some policemen even dressed up in women's clothing and posed as prostitutes to see if the killer approached them. However, in this age before forensic science and fingerprinting, the only way to catch the killer was to see them commit murder or get someone to own up!

The witnesses

For the police, hope rested with the witnesses who claimed to have been near one of the murder scenes on the night of the killing. But had they seen the killer or just an innocent person walking the streets?

Look carefully at **Source B**. It is a summary of each of the witness statements in the investigation. The source gives witnesses' names, the murder scenes they were near, what they saw and when. Read each report carefully – later on you will be asked to work out what Jack the Ripper might have looked like.

Be a Top Historian

Good historians can use **evidence** to investigate questions, such as what Jack the Ripper looked like. Comparing witness statements to find ways they agree or disagree is called **cross-referencing**.

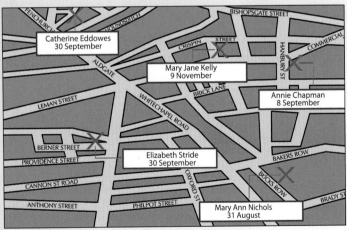

SOURCE A: *A map of the Whitechapel area of London's East End showing where each victim was found. The maze-like streets were full of pubs, houses for rent and cheap 'doss houses' where a bed in a room cost a few pennies per week.*

Hungry for More?

Over the years, many writers and historians have claimed to have worked out who the real Ripper was… but no one has ever proved anything. There have been dozens of suspects… so why not try to find out about some of them? Try searching for M J Druitt, Aaron Kosminski, Frances Tumblety and William Sickert.

Name of witness	Near to which scene was the Ripper seen?	Time of sighting	What did the Ripper look like?
Emily Walter	Annie Chapman	2:00am	Foreigner aged 37, dark beard and moustache. Wearing short dark jacket, dark vest and trousers, black scarf and black felt hat.
Elizabeth Long	Annie Chapman	5:30am	Dark complexion, brown deerstalker hat, possibly a dark overcoat. Aged over 40, somewhat taller than Chapman. A foreigner.
J Best and John Gardner	Elizabeth Stride	11:00pm	5'5" tall, English, black moustache, blond eyelashes, weak, wearing a suit and a hat.
William Marshall	Elizabeth Stride	11:45pm	Small, black coat, dark trousers, middle aged, round cap with a small sailor-like peak. 5'6", stout, appearance of a clerk. No moustache, no gloves, with a coat.
Matthew Packer	Elizabeth Stride	12:00–12:30pm	Aged 25–30, clean-shaven and respectable appearance, 5'7", hard, dark, felt deerstalker hat, dark clothes. Carrying a newspaper parcel 18 x 7 inches.
James Brown	Elizabeth Stride	12:45am	5'7", stout, long black coat reaching almost to his heels.
Israel Schwartz	Elizabeth Strid	12:45am	First man: Aged 30, 5'5", brown haired, fair complexion, small brown moustache, full face, broad shoulders, dark jacket and trousers, black cap with peak. Second man: Aged 35, 5'11", fresh complexion, light brown hair, dark overcoat, old, black, hard felt hat with a wide brim, clay pipe.
Joseph Lawende	Catherine Eddowes	1:30am	Aged 30, 5'7", fair complexion, brown moustache, coat, red neckerchief, grey peaked cloth cap. Sailor-like.
James Blenkingsop	Catherine Eddowes	1:30am	Well dressed.
Mary Ann Cox	Mary Kelly	11:45pm	Short, stout man, shabbily-dressed. Hat, blotchy face, carroty moustache, holding can of beer.
George Hutchinson	Mary Kelly	2:00am	Aged 34–35, 5'6", pale complexion, dark hair, slight moustache curled at each end, long dark coat, dark jacket underneath. Light waistcoat, thick gold chain with a red stone seal, dark trousers and button boots, gaiters, white buttons. White shirt; black tie fastened with a horseshoe pin. Dark hat turned down in middle. Red handkerchief. Jewish and respectable in appearance.

SOURCE B: *This is a summary of each of the witness statements in the 'Jack the Ripper' murder investigation.*

Work

1 The following eight events have all been mixed up. Put them in the correct chronological order:
- Murder of Elizabeth Stride.
- Second 'Dear Boss' letter arrives.
- Murder of Mary Kelly.
- Murder of Mary Ann Nichols.
- Police receive letter and human body parts through the post.
- Murder of Annie Chapman.
- Murder of Catherine Eddowes.
- First 'Dear Boss' letter arrives.

2 Now it's time to be a History Mystery Detective by looking at lots of different clues about what the murderer might have looked like. Look at **Source B**. As you can see from the wide variety of descriptions, the job of narrowing down the search for the Ripper by working out what he looked like was a very

difficult one. However, there are enough similarities in some of the witness statements to give us a good idea, or a 'best fit', as to what the Ripper might have looked like. Using the witness statements, design a 'WANTED' poster for Jack the Ripper.
- Draw a full length 'artist's impression' of Jack the Ripper.
- Include a BEWARE file warning the public what to watch out for: physical appearance, usual clothing, approximate age, 'killing time', favourite 'haunts' and any other useful information.

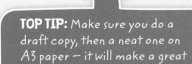

TOP TIP: Make sure you do a draft copy, then a neat one on A3 paper — it will make a great class display.

During the 1600s, Britain became a powerful trading nation. Goods such as sugar, cotton and tobacco flooded into the country and items made in Britain were shipped to faraway places. Many British people became rich as a result of this. But there was a dark side to this trade… the trade in human beings. So how exactly did the 'slave trade' work? How, and why, did it start? And to what extent was Britain involved?

What is 'trade'?

'Trade' means to buy and sell 'goods'. And it's possible for people (traders) to make a fortune from 'trading'. Trading had been big business for years before the 1700s – British ships carried British goods (like wool, corn and chains) to other countries and sold them. Then traders loaded their ships with goods that were popular in Britain (like tea, sugar, tobacco and cotton) and sold them to the British.

So what was the 'slave trade'?

The slave trade is when human beings are bought and sold (instead of goods). The idea of slavery is a very old one. For thousands of years, men have captured 'weaker' people, treated them as their own property and forced them to do their work. The Egyptians used slaves to build the pyramids (see **Source A**) and the Romans forced slaves to fight in gladiator arenas for entertainment. But from around 1500 onwards, slavery turned into a profitable international business that earned people millions, but forced others to move to the other side of the world and live their lives as slaves.

Why were the slaves needed?

In the 1500s, lots of people left Europe to settle in the newly discovered continents of North and South America. Many were farmers who grew crops that were very popular in Europe – like cotton, tobacco, sugar and coffee – and they sold them for high prices. To begin with, some farmers forced local tribesmen to do the farming for them, but some local tribes ran off, and others died out from disease or cruelty (see **Source B**). And when they ran out of local slaves, the European settlers had to go elsewhere to find new ones: Africa.

The slave trade triangle

African slaves ended up in North and South America and the West Indies as a result of a three-legged trading journey known as the **slave trade triangle** (see **Source C**).

SOURCE A: *Slaves being used in Ancient Egypt to build the pyramids.*

SOURCE B: *An image from 1595 showing Spanish settlers slaughtering or capturing natives in South America to work as slaves.*

SOURCE C: *The slave trade triangle.*

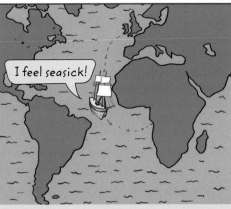

1 In Europe (in Britain, Spain or France, for example) a group of rich businessmen would get together and buy (or rent) a ship.

2 They load the ship with goods popular in Africa – cloth, guns, iron pots and pans, cheap bracelets, swords, kettles, alcohol – and set sail.

3 They sail the loaded ship to the African coast.

4 They unload the ship and exchange the goods for captured slaves. The slave trader swaps a cheap load of goods for something that is really needed in the Americas… slaves.

5 The ship is loaded with the slaves and they are taken on a two-month journey across the Atlantic Ocean. The second part of the ship's journey is known as 'The Middle Passage'.

6 Once the slaves arrive in North America, South America or the West Indies, they are cleaned up and sold to farmers.

7 The slaves go off to work for the farmers and the slave traders will buy a load of sugar, cotton or tobacco and load it onto their empty ship.

8 The loaded ship then completes the third part of its journey back to Europe. The whole journey might take six months.

9 The slave traders sell their cargo to the cotton-wearing, sugar-loving, tobacco-smoking public… and make another huge profit.

Work

1 In your own words, explain the difference between 'trade', 'slave' and the 'slave trade'.

OR: Create a diagram or poster explaining how the slave trade worked.

2 Why did European settlers in North and South America and the West Indies want slaves?

3 **EITHER**: Explain how the slave trade was organized in your own words.

4 a Why was the slave trade so profitable?

b The slave trade is often referred to as 'triangular trade' or 'the slave triangle'. How do you think it got its name?

When did the British get involved?

From the 1560s onwards, British traders got involved in the slave trade. One slave trader, John Hawkins, made so much money that he asked Queen Elizabeth I herself if he could include his new money-making scheme on his family's coat of arms! **Source A** shows his family crest. Today, Hawkins is sometimes called 'the father of the slave trade'.

Slaves on British farms in America

In the 1600s, thousands of British people left Britain to settle in America. In fact, at this time much of the eastern side of America was run by the British. The settlers were mainly farmers, growing tobacco, cotton and other crops. Historians think that the first slaves to work on the settlers' farms over in America arrived from Africa in 1619 (see **Source B**). In total, around 11,000 British ships took millions of slaves to America.

How profitable was slavery?

Britain wasn't the only European nation to get involved in slavery… but Britain made some of the largest profits. And all sorts of people were involved. Queen Elizabeth I, for example, was a business partner of John Hawkins – and King Charles II was a partner in the Royal African Company, a slave trading business that transported 60,000 slaves from Africa between 1680 and 1688. Many of the slaves were **branded** with the letters 'DY' when they were captured – after the man who ran the company, James, Duke of York (King Charles II's brother, who later became King James II).

SOURCE B: *African slaves being brought ashore in America, 1619.*

▼ **SOURCE C:** *A 1634 painting of Princess Henrietta, the youngest daughter of King Charles I of England. Black servants, brought to England as slaves, often appeared in paintings at this time. In some paintings they are grouped with the family's pets or horses, a sign of their status in the house.*

SOURCE A:
John Hawkins' coat of arms.

Slavery in Britain

An estimated three million African slaves were bought and sold between the early 1600s and 1807, generating profits of about £12 million (equivalent to more than £1 billion today). This money made Britain one of the richest and most powerful nations in the world. Many of the fine buildings in Liverpool and Bristol (and also London to some extent) were built on the profits of slavery (see **Source D**). Even Penny Lane – the Liverpool street made famous by the 1967 Beatles' hit – is thought to have been named after a slave ship owner named James Penny! And in 1785, a well-known British actor, George F. Cooke, said, 'Every brick in the city of Liverpool is cemented with the blood of a slave.'

In fact, many Britons played a significant part in the slave trade – ship owners (who allowed their ships to be used), bankers (who lent them the money), investors (who shared in the profits) and importers (who brought in the goods that slaves farmed). Yet Britain's link to slavery goes even further. For example, the world-famous National Gallery in London received its first major donation of paintings from a man who had built up his art collection with the money he made from slave dealing. And several men who ran the Bank of England in the early years were involved in slavery too.

> '*If our slave trade had gone,*
>
> *There's an end to our lives,*
>
> *Beggars all we must be,*
>
> *Our children and wives.*'

SOURCE E: *A well-known rhyme of the 1700s.*

SOURCE D: *Liverpool Town Hall (opened in 1754) was paid for by Liverpool businessmen who had made money from the slave trade. In fact, 20 of Liverpool's mayors between 1787 and 1807 are thought to have been slave traders.*

Work

1 Make a list of ways Britain was linked to the slave trade. The links could be through the Royal Family, British cities, slave traders or bankers, for example.

2 Look at **Source A**. Whose coat of arms was this and why do you think he decided to add a slave at the top of the shield?

3 Look at **Source C**. Why do you think Princess Henrietta wanted the slave included in her portrait?

4 Look through the text to find the quote from George F. Cooke. What do you think he meant?

5 Look at **Source E**. In your opinion, is the writer of this rhyme for or against the slave trade? Give reasons for your answer.

What was it like on a slave ship?

At the height of the slave trade, in the 1700s, an estimated six million Africans were taken across the Atlantic Ocean to work as slaves. Over 50,000 voyages, lasting between 40 and 70 days, were made in the 300 years between 1510 and 1833. But what was the journey like? How were the slaves treated? And how do we know about these terrible voyages? Your challenge is to work out the answers to these questions. Look through all the sources carefully before beginning the tasks in the Work section.

Mission Objective

- Examine sources in order to understand what conditions were like on a slave ship.

SOURCE A: *This eighteenth-century illustration shows slaves being loaded on board a ship for an Atlantic crossing.*

Slaves were shackled together in rows, lying either on their backs or on their sides (like spoons).

This plan shows 454 slaves on board, but slave ships (depending on their size) could carry anything from 250 to 600 slaves. We know so much about some slave ships (like the *Brookes*) because their owners kept detailed records of their journeys. After all, the slave trade made big money – and it was totally legal – so traders treated their job like any other professional business.

Slaves were given space of 1.8m length by 0.4m width to lie in.

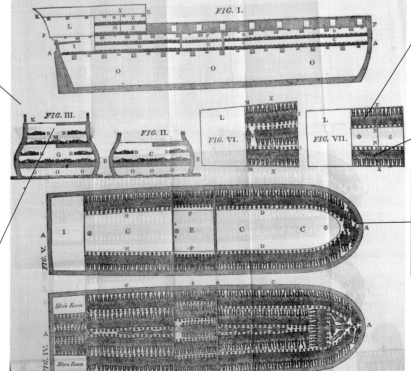

There was approximately 1.5m between the slave decks.

Men were loaded into the bow (front of the ship), boys in the centre, and women and young girls in the stern (back of the ship).

SOURCE B: *A plan from the slave ship* Brookes *showing how slaves were packed onto it.*

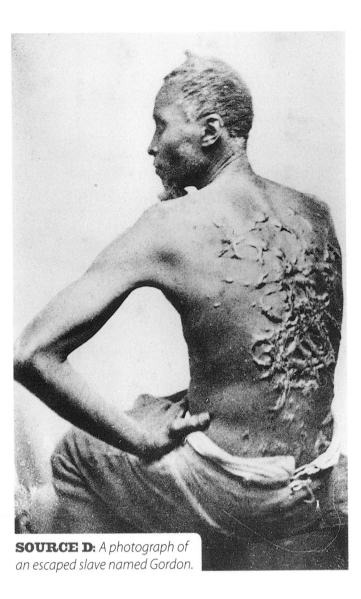

SOURCE D: *A photograph of an escaped slave named Gordon.*

Slave rebellion

Some slaves joined together and started rebellions. In 1791, a **revolt** started on the island of Saint-Domingue in the West Indies. The slaves, led by a man called Toussaint L'Ouverture, set fire to the sugar cane fields and murdered their white masters. First, they defeated British troops sent to sort out the trouble… and then a French army. In 1804, the 'free' slaves renamed their island. They called it Haiti. This was the first island run by former black slaves in the West Indies. Perhaps others would follow…

Work

1 **a** What sorts of jobs would slaves do:
      i   out in the fields?
      ii in the plantation owner's house?
   b Why do you think slave owners treated slaves so brutally, especially when they tried to escape?
   c As a slave, write a diary entry of no more than 250 words, describing a day in your life. What do you do? How are you treated?

2 Look at **Source A**.
   a Describe what it shows.
   b The working conditions in this picture don't appear to be that bad. What could explain this?

3 Look at **Source E**.
   a Why were reward posters like this produced?
   b Why do you think the owner believes the runaway slave will look for a job on a steamboat?
   c The owner asks that this slave is returned so that he 'can use him again'. What is the owner worried about? Look at **Sources C** and **D** before writing your answer.

4 **a** What effect do you think the revolt in Saint-Domingue would have had on slave owners in other countries? Explain your answer carefully.
   b Why do you think Haiti is a very special island to many Africans, even today?

$150 REWARD

RUNAWAY SLAVE – left on the night of the 2nd

A negro man, who calls himself HENRY MAY, about 22 years old, 5 feet 6 or 8 inches tall, ordinary colour, chunky build, bushy head and has it divided mostly on one side, keeps it very nicely combed, has been raised in the house and is a first-rate dining room servant. Worked in a tavern in Louisville for 18 months. I expect he has gone back there.

He may try to get employment on a steamboat. He is a good cook and is very handy. When he left, he was wearing a dark red coat, dark red trousers, new – he had other clothes too.

50 dollar reward if taken in Louisville, 100 dollars if taken one hundred miles from Louisville but still in this state, and 150 dollars if taken out of this state, and delivered to me, or secured in jail so that I can use him again.

WILLIAM BURKE
Bardstown, Kentucky, 3 September, 1838

SOURCE E: *A copy of a reward poster for an escaped slave. Although it was dangerous, thousands of slaves fled to states in the United States that had already freed slaves.*

What Happened When?
1791
1791, the year of the slave revolt in Saint-Domingue, is when the earliest known reference to the game of baseball was written.

Why was slavery abolished?

In 1807, the British Parliament did a remarkable thing – it **abolished** the slave trade (see **Source A**). In other words, it made it illegal to buy and sell slaves… but people were allowed to keep the slaves they already owned! In 1833, Parliament banned slave ownership too – not only in Britain but throughout the **British Empire**. So why did Parliament do this? Why was slavery – a business that made so much money for so many people – banned? And what were the most important factors that played a part in ending slavery?

Mission Objectives

- Explain when both slave trading and slave ownership ended in Britain and the Empire.
- Outline the different factors that contributed to the abolition of slavery.
- Prioritize the different factors that led to the abolition of slavery.

The beginning of the end

Britain had been involved in the slave trade for hundreds of years. It was not illegal to make money from it and all sorts of people were involved. Even King Charles II was a partner in a slave trading business! But some people felt slavery was wrong – and by the late 1700s a campaign had been started to get the slave trade banned. This 'anti-slavery' group was very important – but was slavery banned *just* because of this group… or were there other reasons why it ended? Your challenge is to look through the following factors very carefully and try to form your own thoughts on what might answer the question 'Why was slavery abolished?'

Factor No.1: Slavery wasn't making as much money as it used to

Some people have argued that the decision to get rid of slavery was made easier for Parliament because the slave trade wasn't making as much money as it used to. In the 1770s, the price of sugar dropped and many British plantations in the West Indies couldn't make a profit and closed down. And with fewer plantations, there wasn't the need for as many slaves. In 1771, plantation owners in Barbados bought 2728 slaves from Africa. The following year they bought none! So with fewer people making enormous profits, there were fewer people to argue in favour of keeping the slave trade. Also, some people claimed that slaves didn't work as hard as people who got paid for their work. They said slaves had no reason to work as hard as possible because they didn't get extra rewards or bonuses. Some people argued that it wasn't good business to have slaves working for you who didn't care about their jobs (see **Source B**).

SOURCE A: *In 2007, a special edition £2 coin was made to commemorate the abolition of the slave trade. Have you ever had one of these coins?*

'The work done by slaves, though it appears to cost only their maintenance [food and shelter], is in the end the most expensive of any. A person who can gain no property can have no other interest but to eat as much and to work as little as possible. Whatever work he does… can be squeezed out of him by violence only.'

SOURCE B: *What the famous economist Adam Smith thought about slavery in 1776.*

Factor No. 2: Slaves helped end slavery!

Other people have argued that it was the actions of the slaves themselves that led to the end of slavery. In 1791, the slaves on Saint-Domingue, a French colony in the Caribbean, rebelled, killed the white plantation owners and set fire to the sugar-cane fields. Led by the inspirational slave Toussaint L'Ouverture, they managed to keep control of the island despite attacks from both French and British soldiers.

In 1804, the island was renamed Haiti, declared independent and outlawed slavery. Plantation owners throughout the West Indies were terrified that the rebellion would spread and their crops would soon be in flames. White slave owners had argued that Africans were inferior to Europeans and that their natural position was to be following orders and doing simple, manual work. What had happened in Haiti had proved to many people that this argument was wrong.

SOURCE C: *The slaves of Saint-Domingue revolting against their French masters. Saint-Domingue was soon renamed Haiti by the former slaves who took control of the island.*

Wise Up Words

abolish   British Empire

Work

1   Write a sentence explaining what the word 'abolish' means.

2 What's the difference between the anti-slavery law passed in 1807 and the one passed in 1833?

3 **a** Look at **Source C**. What do you think is happening?
   b The BBC named Toussaint L'Ouverture as an 'unsung hero of abolition'. Why do you think it gave him this title?

Be a Top Historian

Top historians know that complex events, such as the end of slavery, have a number of complex **causes** (or factors). Sometimes causes are not equally important (that's for *you* to judge), but the causes of an event are often linked.

Why was slavery abolished?

Factor No.3: Black people proved the racists wrong!

There were all sorts of people – doctors, businessmen, lawyers – who thought that slavery was perfectly acceptable. In fact, some said that slavery was a good thing because it gave Africans something useful to do – and it meant that they could be taught about Christianity at the same time (see **Sources A**, **B** and **C**).

'Look at the Negro, so well known to you. Is he shaped like any white person? Is the anatomy of his frame or his muscles, or his organs like ours? Does he walk like us? Not in the least. What a hatred the white people have for him. Can the blacks become civilized? I should say not.'

SOURCE B: *Adapted from* The Races of Men *by Dr Robert Knox, 1850.*

'The negroes of Africa, when they are in Africa, are useless. They never improve themselves or learn about art or science. The only way to improve them is to make them useful and happy by making them work hard.'

▲ **SOURCE A:** *Adapted from a letter published in* Gentleman's Magazine, *23 April 1789.*

'God says that slavery is right, so it is wrong to stop it. It makes the African happy, so it would be cruel to end it.'

▲ **SOURCE C:** *Written by a Scottish lawyer in 1790.*

But slaves who lived in Britain (who had been brought here by slave traders) got a chance to prove the racist attitudes wrong! In Britain, there were no laws that said slavery was illegal… but there were no laws to say it was *legal* either. So some slaves, helped out by lawyers who were against slavery, went to court to claim their freedom. More and more judges, impressed by the slaves' arguments, allowed them to go free. And some former slaves went even further.

One former slave, Olaudah Equiano, campaigned tirelessly to convince British people that the slave trade was wrong. He had been taken from his home in Africa to Barbados when he was just 11 years old. He worked as a servant to a ship's captain, travelled widely, and learned to read and write while staying in England. He was then taken to North America and sold once more but, through incredible hard work and patience, he bought his freedom and moved back to Britain, where he wrote his life story and got married. This was widely read and turned many people in Britain against slavery. The fact that he was clearly intelligent and articulate made a nonsense out of the claims that Africans were inferior and only good for manual work.

SOURCE D: *Equiano's tales of cruelty and inhumanity changed the attitudes of many people in Britain towards the slave trade.*

Factor No.4: The anti-slavery campaigners

Some people believe it was the actions of religious Europeans that ended slavery. Granville Sharp, for example, helped former slaves in court cases against their old masters and helped bring the injustice of slavery to the British public's attention. In 1787, a group of 12 Christian men, including William Wilberforce, formed a group to fight for abolition. Wilberforce was an MP and made speeches against slavery in Parliament. Thomas Clarkson collected together evidence of the horrors of the **Middle Passage** and the treatment that slaves faced. The campaigners, who all believed that slavery went against the teachings of Christ, then used this evidence to collect huge petitions from the public.

> 'The grand object of my parliamentary existence is the abolition of the slave trade. Before this great cause all others dwindle in my eyes. If it pleases God to honour me so far, may I be the instrument of stopping such a course of wickedness and cruelty as never before disgraced a Christian country.'

SOURCE F: *From the writings of William Wilberforce, 1796.*

SOURCE G: *The pottery manufacturer Josiah Wedgwood was a supporter of the campaign to abolish slavery and a good friend of Thomas Clarkson. In 1787, he began producing these small pottery medallions to convince people that slavery was wrong. Over 200,000 were made in total and the logo 'Am I not a man and a brother?' appeared on dinner plates, bracelets and brooches.*

FACT!

When slave ownership ended in the British Empire in 1833, the government paid out £20 million to former slave owners for their 'loss of property'. And the list of people who received compensation was very interesting – the Bishop of Exeter, for example, received over £12,000 for the loss of 665 slaves he owned with his business partners in the West Indies!

Middle Passage

SOURCE E: *William Wilberforce is buried in Westminster Abbey, London. Here, Queen Elizabeth II lays a wreath on a statue of him to commemorate 200 years since the abolition of slavery in 2007.*

Work

1 Look at **Sources A**, **B** and **C**.
   a What is meant by the term 'politically incorrect'? You might want to discuss this with a partner or with the class.
   b Make a list of all the politically incorrect attitudes you can find in these sources.
   c Do you think these attitudes might explain the way slaves were treated? Explain your answer.

2 a Write down these three statements as headings:
   • 'Slavery was abolished because it wasn't making as much money as it used to.'
   • 'The slaves themselves ended slavery.'
   • 'Religious campaigners in Britain brought an end to the slave trade.'
   Under each heading, write down all the evidence you can find on pages 88–91 to support the statement.
   b So, in your opinion, why do you think Britain ended its role in the slave trade? Write an extended answer, making sure you explain what you think were the most important reasons.

3 Look at **Source G**. Design your own medallion that campaigns for the abolition of slavery. Remember to include an eye-catching image and slogan. Perhaps plan this activity in a small group or with a partner.

Britain versus France... in North America

In the 1600s, settlers from lots of different European countries sailed over to the newly discovered continent of North America. People from Spain, France, Britain, Holland, Sweden and Finland all arrived hoping to start a new life and make their fortune. But there were more British and French settlers than from any other country so, as you'd expect, they tried to grab the most land. And when both Britain and France wanted the same piece of land, you can guess what happened, can't you? So where did the British and the French clash? Who won the war? And what impact did the fighting have on each country?

Mission Objectives

- Outline where European settlement occurred in North America.
- Explain how Britain came to dominate the continent.

Land grab

The British grabbed lots of land, stretching over 1600km, along the east coast of North America. They split themselves up into separate areas, or colonies, and farmed the land, growing cotton, tobacco, corn, oats, potatoes, wheat and barley. The French occupied a lot of land in the northern part of North America (now known as Canada) and inland around the Mississippi and St Lawrence rivers.

Both the French and the British were well armed, and built forts to guard their land. The Spanish had claimed land in North America too, down in the south (see **Source A**).

French territory
Great Lakes/St Lawrence River

Settlements such as Quebec, Montreal and Detroit contained farmers, traders and fishermen.

French forts

A string of forts stretched from French territory in the south up to the north.

New Orleans area

Lots of French settlers here.

Hudson Bay
A few hundred British hunters lived in this vast area.

British colonies
New England

Farmers, fishermen and shipbuilders.

Middle colonies

The Dutch settled here but the British took their land. Still, a large Dutch population mixed with the British. Lots of farmers, traders and businessmen. A growing number of rich towns.

Southern colonies

Rich farmers with huge estates growing cotton and tobacco. Slaves brought over from Africa to work on the farms.

Quebec
A large, important town in French territory. Founded by the French in 1608.

Florida
A Spanish colony.

Spanish territory
The Spanish had controlled this land for a long time, but were probably unwilling to go north as they believed there was no gold there.

N

0 _____ 500 Km

St Lawrence
Ohio
Mississippi

SOURCE A: *A map showing how land in North America was roughly divided up between the British and the French (and the Spanish) in the 1600s.*

FACT!

When the European settlers went to America, there were tribes – **Native Americans** – already there. Obviously there was conflict between them – the tribes saw the settlers as **invaders**, while the settlers felt they had a right to live wherever they wanted. In the British areas of North America, for example, the settlers usually drove the tribes away and destroyed the forests so they could farm the land. The tribes then moved further inland onto the vast plains of North America.

On the warpath

By 1750, it was beginning to look like the British and the French in North America were soon going to fight. The French wanted the rich farmland that the British had developed near the east coast… and the British wanted to expand into French land so they could set up more farms. In 1754, the French built a new fort *very* close to British territory. The consequences of this would lead to a war between Britain and France known as the **Seven Years War**. Read through the story in **Source B** on pages 93 and 94 carefully to see who won.

Work

1 Why do you think settlers from European nations were so keen to settle in North America?

2 Look at **Source A**. In your own words, describe how the land in North America was divided up between different European countries.

3 a What is a Native American?

  b Why do you think there was conflict between Native Americans and European settlers?

SOURCE B: *The Seven Years War.*

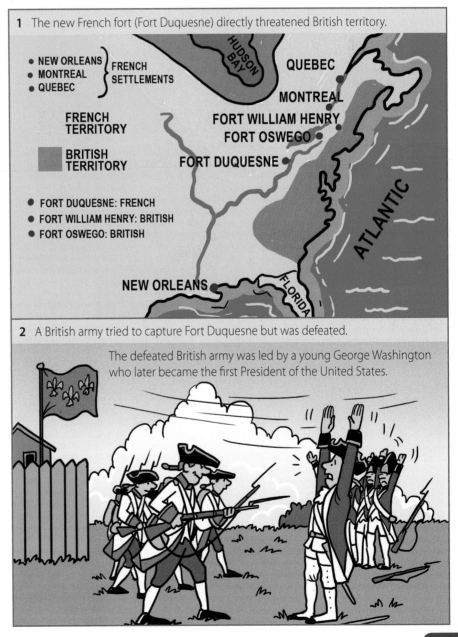

1 The new French fort (Fort Duquesne) directly threatened British territory.

- NEW ORLEANS ⎫
- MONTREAL ⎬ FRENCH SETTLEMENTS
- QUEBEC ⎭

FRENCH TERRITORY

BRITISH TERRITORY

- FORT DUQUESNE: FRENCH
- FORT WILLIAM HENRY: BRITISH
- FORT OSWEGO: BRITISH

HUDSON BAY — QUEBEC — MONTREAL — FORT WILLIAM HENRY — FORT OSWEGO — FORT DUQUESNE — ATLANTIC — NEW ORLEANS — FLORIDA

2 A British army tried to capture Fort Duquesne but was defeated.

The defeated British army was led by a young George Washington who later became the first President of the United States.

3 The French then captured two British forts (Oswego and William Henry). The French were now set for an all-out attack on British territory. War was officially declared in May 1756.

4 Meanwhile, the British Prime Minister (William Pitt) had sent lots of troops over to North America to defend British territory. The troops arrived just in time.

5 In 1758, the British forts of Oswego and William Henry were recaptured and the French Fort Duquesne was captured too (it was renamed 'Fort Pitt' in the Prime Minister's honour).

The French were no longer a threat to British territory… so the British went on the attack!

6 In September 1759, the British decided to attack the French city of Quebec.

The French thought the city was impossible to attack… but James Wolfe, a talented young general leading the British, had a plan!

7 Under cover of darkness, James Wolfe led 5000 men in rowing boats down the river where they silently climbed the steep cliffs to launch a surprise dawn raid on the French (see **Source A**).

The British captured Quebec, but Wolfe was wounded and died soon after. The French commander, Montcalm, was also killed.

8 Soon the British captured all the French forts and settlements, including Montreal.

A treaty, signed in Paris, gave French land in North America to Britain (except New Orleans). Britain also gained French territory in the Caribbean. Britain also gained Florida from Spain (which had fought with the French).

A real victory?

Although Britain defeated France and took over its land in North America, the French were always looking for revenge against the British… and they would soon get their chance! Twelve years later, the people who lived in America decided they no longer wanted to be part of Britain. They decided that, despite being British and speaking English, they wanted to break free from British rule, run themselves and not pay taxes to Britain. In short, they wanted their **independence**, so the British sent over troops to control these rebels. And guess which country was only too happy to help the rebels fight the British troops? That's right, France!

The First World War

It wasn't just Britain and France that fought each other in the Seven Years War. Austria, Russia and Sweden helped out France while Portugal and areas in what we now call Germany supported Britain. And fighting took place in other areas of the world where these countries had land, such as in the Caribbean, Africa and India. For these reasons, some historians (including Winston Churchill) called the Seven Years War the 'First World War'!

Wise Up Words

independence

Work

1 Read the full story of the Seven Years War on pages 93 and 94.
   a Describe the role played in the war by the following:
   • George Washington
   • William Pitt
   • James Wolfe.
   b What was agreed at the Treaty of Paris in 1763?
2 Do you think some modern historians are right to describe the Seven Years War as a 'World War'? Give reasons for your answer.
3 Imagine you are a script-writer in Hollywood, and you've written a script for a film about the Seven Years War. Write a pitch to a film company to persuade them to make your film. What elements of the story would you emphasize?

SOURCE A: *British soldiers, in red, climb the steep cliffs in order to capture Quebec.*

In what way is the execution of a French king linked to Britain?

Look at **Source A**. It is a French engraving from 1793. Look at the machine that's just been used to cut off the man's head. It's called a **guillotine** and was used many hundreds of times during this period of French history. A guillotine consists of a tall frame in which a heavy, sharp blade is placed. When the blade is released it drops down and chops off a person's head. The executed man pictured in **Source A** is a French king, Louis XVI. So why did he have his head chopped off? What events led up to this moment? What happened in France after the execution of their king? And what had a war between Britain and France over in North America got to do with all this?

Mission Objectives

- Recall why the French Revolution took place.
- Discover how the war in North America between Britain and France was connected to the French Revolution.

Britain versus France

For seven years, between 1756 and 1763, Britain and France were at war over who should control North America. Britain won the Seven Years War… but the French wanted revenge!

Britain versus… America!

In 1775, the people who lived in some of the settlements along the east coast of America (who were officially British) decided they no longer wanted to be part of Britain. They saw themselves as 'Americans' and were fed up with British controls and laws. Also, they had to pay taxes to Britain, which they felt was unfair. So the British sent troops over to fight these American 'rebels'. This is known as the **American War of Independence**… and the French helped out the rebels with troops and supplies. Against all odds, the rebels (helped by France) beat the British. In 1781, the British surrendered (see **Source B**) and left the Americans to rule themselves. In 1783, the area officially became known as the United States of America.

SOURCE A: *The execution of King Louis XVI in 1793.*

Impact on France

The French were on the winning side in the war (and they'd finally beaten the British), but the war cost the French a fortune. As a result, the French king increased taxes to pay for it… and the poor French people were furious.

Also, the ordinary French citizens had seen how the Americans had got rid of their British rulers and set up their own government. This inspired them. So in 1789, the unhappy, hungry and poor French people began a rebellion against the king and all his rich followers. It would become known as the **French Revolution**.

SOURCE B: *A famous painting showing the British (in red) surrendering to the leaders of the American and French armies (Washington and Lafayette) in October 1781.*

Wise Up Words

American War of Independence   French Revolution
guillotine

What Happened When?

1783

In 1783, the year that the 'United States of America' was officially established, two Frenchmen launched the world's first hydrogen-filled balloon, *Le Globe*, in Paris.

Work

1 a What does the word 'independence' mean?
  b In your own words, explain why the French helped American rebels to fight the British.

2 What was the impact of the American War of Independence on:
  • Britain
  • France?

3 Look at **Source B**. Explain why the British army leader is surrendering to both the American and French armies.

In what way is the execution of a French king linked to Britain?

The French Revolution

In July 1789, an angry mob of starving peasants broke into a huge royal prison in the centre of Paris, called the Bastille (see **Source A**). Soon there were riots all over France as local people took over control of different areas. The king, Louis XVI, had little choice but to give up some of his powers and the country was run by a National Assembly (a sort of Parliament). The new rulers famously published a list of 'rights' that they believed people should have to make France a better place. In years to come, many countries all over the world would use the list when deciding how their countries should be run (see **Source B**).

War and execution

At this time, thousands of rich French people ran away from France to other European countries. They urged other countries to help them end the revolution. Back in France, these people were accused of being 'enemies of the revolution'. In April 1792, the new French government declared war on some of these countries – Austria and Prussia. Soon after, in a move that astonished (and worried) many of Europe's leaders, the French executed their king… and his wife. In fact, the rulers of Britain, Austria, Prussia (now part of Germany), Holland and Spain were afraid that the revolution might spread to their countries too. Lots of other rich Frenchmen who had dared to stay were also killed. This became known as the **Reign of Terror**. In 1793, French troops invaded Belgium – and then declared war on Britain and Holland. Spain and Portugal declared war on France too.

The Declaration of the Rights of Man

- All men are born and remain free and equal in rights.
- Governments should always try to preserve these rights.
- No one should be punished except by laws set up before the offence was committed.
- Every man is presumed innocent until proven guilty.
- No one should be picked on for his opinions or religious beliefs.
- Every citizen may speak, write and print freely.
- Taxation should be fair and based on what people can afford to pay.
- No one can have their property taken away for no good reason.

▲ **SOURCE B:** *Some of the ideas contained in the **Declaration of the Rights of Man**. Unfortunately, these rights only applied to men – women would have to wait for many years until they got equal rights in various countries.*

SOURCE A: *An angry French mob storms the Bastille on 14 July 1789. Every year this date is celebrated in France as a national holiday.*

Britain stands alone

By 1796, all of the countries except Britain had been beaten by the French. In fact, the French seemed unbeatable on land… and Britain only remained unbeaten because it had a brilliant navy to defend the coast. Then, the defeated Dutch and Spanish joined forces with France and vowed to attack Britain – and then they had a larger *combined* navy than the British! So it seemed that an invasion of Britain was inevitable! And to make matters even worse, a remarkable new military commander had taken control of the French army and was winning stunning victories. His name was Napoleon Bonaparte.

Wise Up Words

Declaration of the Rights of Man
Reign of Terror

SOURCE C: *A painting of the French defeat of the Austrians at the Battle of Neresheim in 1796.*

FACT!

In 1798, a group of Irishmen, fed up with being part of Britain, launched an uprising hoping to break free from British rule. French troops even helped the Irish and landed troops on the west coast of Ireland. However, despite early victories, the French and Irish were eventually defeated… and Ireland remained under British control.

Be a Top Historian

Events, such as the French Revolution and Britain's war against France (and Holland and Spain), can have both short- and long-term causes. Why not discuss the short- and long-term causes of these events?

Work

1 Look at **Source A**.
   a Describe what's happening in the picture.
   b Why do you think this event is celebrated in France every year?

2 Look at **Source B**. Why has this 'declaration' been seen as so significant in the years since it was written?

3 Put these events in the correct chronological order.
   • France invades Belgium and declares war on Britain
   • French King executed
   • French defeat all nations except Britain
   • Declaration of Rights of Man published
   • French king gives up his power
   • Holland and Spain join France against Britain

4 In your own words, explain how the execution of a French king is linked to Britain.

Towards the end of the eighteenth century, the French people rebelled against their royal rulers and executed their king (and many of his supporters). This was deeply worrying for many people in Britain – especially King George III! What if the ideas of the French Revolution caught on in Britain? This fear and mistrust between the two countries soon led to war. Other countries, afraid the revolution might spread to them, decided to fight the French too. It was during this time of war that a brilliant French soldier became both famous and feared throughout Europe. In fact, he was so feared in Britain that mothers threatened their poorly behaved children with the phrase 'Little Boney will get you!' So who was 'Little Boney'? And why did the British fear him so much? Why was he so well known?

Mission Objectives

- Outline the key events in Napoleon's wars.
- Assess the impact of Napoleon's campaigns in Europe.

Who was 'Little Boney'?

'Little Boney' was the nickname for Napoleon Bonaparte, the man in charge of the French army. He was given the nickname by British newspapers, which made fun of his size (he was 1.7m tall – not *that* short at the time!) to make him seem less powerful. However, he was a superb military leader. Read about his impressive rise to power.

1 Napoleon was born in 1769 on the island of Corsica, which belonged to France. In 1779, he was sent to French military school. He was bullied because of his Corsican accent but was a good student and joined the French army aged just 16.

2 The French Revolution caused many of the rich officers to leave the army, which meant Napoleon was quickly promoted. In 1793, he was promoted after leading an attack against the French king's supporters and in 1795 he improved his reputation by restoring order in Paris when more royal supporters rebelled.

3 In 1796, he married Joséphine de Beauharnais, a friend of a government minister. He was promoted again and placed in charge of the whole French army.

4 Napoleon reorganized the French Army and inspired it to victories over Austria and Italy. He invaded Egypt in 1798 in an attempt to cut off Britain from its colonies in India but his ships were destroyed by the British navy. He returned to Paris in 1799… still a hero, though!

5 When he returned to France he saw that the country was in crisis. There were food shortages, problems in the government and little money left for war. So Napoleon decided to take over France himself in November 1799.

6 At first he was known as 'First Consul of France', but in 1804 he crowned himself emperor. He introduced some new laws and systems that France still uses today. As he became stronger and won more victories, he placed his relatives on the thrones of Holland, Italy and Spain.

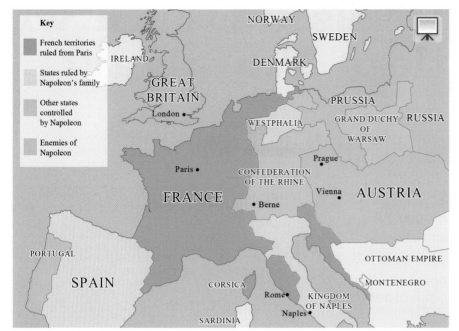

Key
- French territories ruled from Paris
- States ruled by Napoleon's family
- Other states controlled by Napoleon
- Enemies of Napoleon

▲ **SOURCE A:** *Napoleon's armies won many famous victories and not since the Romans had a single state controlled so much of Europe. It was his ambition to unite Europe with a single currency, law and system of weights and measures. Some people have called him the first European!*

JOHN·BULL *offering Little* BONEY *fair play.*

You're a'coming? — You be d—nd! If you mean to invade us, why make such a rout? I say, Little Boney, why don't you come out? yes, d—n'ye, why don't you come out?

I'm a coming! I'm a'coming!!!

SOURCE B: *This cartoon from 1803 shows Britain as 'John Bull' standing in the Channel asking 'Little Boney' for a fight. The idea was to make people less scared of Napoleon.*

FACT!

Napoleon used to disguise himself in peasant clothes and walk around Paris asking questions. He did this to see how well his ideas were being received by the ordinary French people!

Work

1 How old was Napoleon when he:
 a went to military school?
 b joined the French army?
 c was promoted for leading an attack against the king's supporters?
 d restored order in Paris during a rebellion?
 e invaded Egypt… but was defeated?
 f took over France?
 g became emperor?

2 Think about Napoleon's career up to 1805. Choose one moment when he was lucky, another time when he showed how clever he was and one moment when he was helped by circumstance. Explain why you made these choices.

3 a Why do you think the British newspapers called him 'Little Boney'?
 b Why do you think British parents threatened their naughty children with 'Little Boney'?

4 a Write ten facts about Napoleon. Pretend you are a French person living at the time when you write your first five facts… but a British person when you are writing your next five facts.
 b How and why are your first five facts different from your final five facts?

5 Look at **Source A**. Write a few sentences explaining why you think some people have called Napoleon the first European.

What Happened When?

1796

In 1796, the year of Napoleon's promotion to leader of the French army, Edward Jenner first used his smallpox vaccine.

How did 'Nelson's touch' win the Battle of Trafalgar?

In 1803, Napoleon Bonaparte gathered 130,000 troops along the French coast. On a clear day, the French soldiers (who had conquered all of Europe) could see Britain across the English Channel. Napoleon only needed to control the Channel, which he called a 'mere ditch', for a few hours so he could transport his enormous army to Britain. All that stood between Britain and the first foreign invasion since 1066 was the Royal Navy. So what (or who) stopped Napoleon? Why didn't the invasion ever happen? And how did the Battle of Trafalgar affect the rest of British history?

Mission Objectives

- Analyse what 'Nelson's touch' was.
- Explain how successful Nelson's tactics were.
- Recognize how and why the battle was commemorated in Britain.

Vice Admiral Horatio Nelson

The man given the job of saving England was Vice Admiral Horatio Nelson (see **Source A**). Born in Norfolk, England, in 1758, he was the sixth of eleven children and joined the Royal Navy at the age of 12! He soon proved himself a natural leader and was made a captain by the age of 20. He had been fighting in the wars against France since 1793 and had won many famous victories – but he lost the sight in his right eye and his right arm in the process! Famous for his bravery and bold tactics, he once ignored orders by putting a telescope to his blind eye and claiming he couldn't see the signal! Nelson soon became a national hero, as popular as a famous footballer or pop star today. He was put in charge of Britain's impressive navy – but knew that if he was to make Britain safe from France, he needed to completely destroy the French navy and gain control of the seas.

When would the French invasion happen?

Between 1803 and 1805, the French troops trained for their invasion of Britain… but Napoleon knew he had to have control of the English Channel before he could sail his soldiers across to Britain. So he *had* to destroy the Royal Navy. However, the British were just as keen to attack the French ships and in October 1805 the two sides eventually met, just off the coast of Spain (see **Sources B** and **C**).

SOURCE A: *Horatio Nelson, Britain's greatest naval hero, painted in 1799.*

SOURCE B: *The red indicates Wellington's troops and other friendly nations, whilst the blue shows the French (led by Napoleon). The Prussians (on Britain's side), led by von Blücher, are shown in yellow. They arrived in the afternoon and helped win the battle.*

Wise Up Words

abdicate artillery exile infantry

Shako: allowed generals to identify different regiments

Bayonet: used during hand-to-hand fighting

Brightly coloured uniform: allowed the generals to see who was on each side

Musket: inaccurate and slow to load

SOURCE C: *A Napoleonic soldier.*

Evidence D

When Wellington's infantry came under heavy fire from French **artillery**, he ordered them to move behind a ridge and lie down in long grass. This caused the French to think they were retreating and allowed the British soldiers to wipe the French out as they came over the ridge.

Evidence E

Napoleon felt ill and decided to leave the battlefield for a lie down. He put Marshal Ney in charge – who had a reputation for making rash decisions.

SOURCE D: *This breast plate gives you some idea of the destructive power of artillery.*

Evidence F

The French infantry advanced in narrow columns that were just six men wide but many rows deep. This meant that only those at the front could fight and most of the men in the column couldn't fire their muskets.

Evidence G

Napoleon put all of his artillery in one place – at the front of his army. This meant they could deliver devastating firepower but couldn't reach all areas of the battlefield.

Evidence H
Wellington inspired his troops by putting himself in the thick of the action and only narrowly avoided being killed several times (see **Source A**).

Evidence J
Marshal Ney saw the British infantry move behind the ridge, assumed they were retreating and sent all of the French cavalry after them. The British soldiers were hiding in the long grass and attacked the French as they came over the ridge.

Evidence I
The Prussian army was rapidly marching to join up with Wellington's soldiers. Napoleon sent 30,000 of his men from the battlefield to try and stop the Prussian advance. They failed and the Prussians were soon at Waterloo, attacking Napoleon.

Evidence K
Wellington knew that time was on his side. He took no risks and waited for the Prussians to arrive – forcing Napoleon to gamble on dangerous attacks.

FACT!
During the battle, a cannonball hit the Earl of Uxbridge as he rode next to the Duke of Wellington. Uxbridge said, 'By God sir, I've lost my leg!', and the Duke replied, 'By God sir, so you have!' The leg was amputated and buried nearby, where it became a popular tourist attraction!

SOURCE A: *When inspecting his troops, Wellington is reported to have said, 'I don't know what effect these men will have upon the enemy, but, by God, they frighten me.'*

SOURCE B: *Many people say that Napoleon wasn't his usual energetic and inspirational self at Waterloo.*

Be a Top Historian

Top historians know the importance of having a **balanced argument**. This means that it's vital to show different points of view or sides to an argument. Here, you are asked not just to think about the British victory at Waterloo being a result of one factor (e.g. Wellington's brilliance), but to think about how Napoleon might have contributed to his defeat too!

FACT!

After the battle, Napoleon was captured and sent into exile on St Helena, a tiny island in the middle of the Atlantic. He remained there until he died in 1821.

Work

1 Write a sentence or two about the following:
   i   Elba
   ii infantry
   iii artillery
   iv the Earl of Uxbridge
   v   St Helena.

Wellington's brilliance	Napoleon's mistakes

2 a Read through each piece of evidence (A–K) and divide your page into two, as shown opposite. If you think a piece of evidence indicates that Wellington won the battle, write a brief description of it in the 'Wellington's brilliance' column. If you think it describes a mistake by Napoleon, write a description in the 'Napoleon's mistakes' column.

   b Do you think there are any other factors, apart from Wellington's brilliance or Napoleon's mistakes, that might have affected the outcome of the battle?

3 To what extent were Napoleon's mistakes responsible for his loss at the Battle of Waterloo? Explain your answer.

TOP TIP: *There are two sides (or maybe more) to this answer. You need to think about:*
- *how Napoleon's mistakes contributed to his defeat*
- *how Wellington's brilliance helped him win*
- *what else might have helped Napoleon lose… or Wellington win.*

7.1 How did Britain get an empire?

An **empire** is a collection of areas of land or even countries that are ruled over and controlled by one leading or 'mother' country. The places controlled by the mother country are usually called **colonies**. Around 100 years ago, Britain ruled the largest empire the world had ever known. It was even bigger than the famous Roman Empire. Britain ruled over 450 million people living in 56 areas (or colonies) around the world. **Source A** shows you how the British Empire grew.

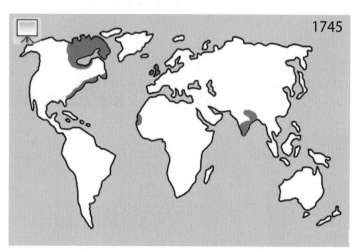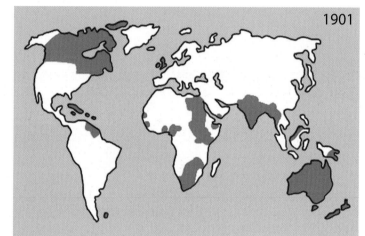

SOURCE A: *The growth of the British Empire from 1745 to 1901. By 1901, Britain's empire contained one quarter of the world's population and covered one quarter of the Earth's total land area.*

Getting an empire

To properly understand the British Empire, it is really important that you learn about two things. Firstly, it is vital that you understand *why* the British wanted such a large empire. Secondly, it is essential that you know *how* Britain got its empire.

So why did Britain want an empire?

There are four reasons why Britain wanted an empire, listed below. Can you match each reason with a source – B, C, D or E?

Britain wanted an empire…

1 To get valuable raw materials and riches
2 So Britain could sell goods to the colonies and make money
3 To become a more powerful country
4 Because Britain thought it was the right thing to do.

'The people of the colonies had to buy goods from Britain. So Britain sold more goods.'

▲ **SOURCE B:** *From a modern history book.*

'The British considered it both a duty and an opportunity to bring Christianity to the "godless" people of newly discovered lands.'

SOURCE C: *Written by Ross Adams, 1992.*

'... countries go "empire-hunting" because they want more resources like grain, cattle, gold, silver, tin or iron. They take over other countries in order to steal all the things they want.'

▲ **SOURCE D:** *Written by a modern historian.*

'The British government used the army and navy to take over land to prevent countries like France and Germany getting it first ... Some places, like Gibraltar, were taken as naval bases.'

SOURCE E: *Written by JoÚ Child, 1992.*

So how did Britain get its empire?

You've investigated *why* Britain wanted an empire, so now it's time to find out *how* Britain got one.

War

If Britain won a war against another country, Britain could often take over any land the other country owned around the world. For example, when Britain won a long war against France, land previously conquered by France became part of the British Empire. That is how Canada and islands in the West Indies such as Tobago and St Lucia became part of the British Empire.

Settlers

Sometimes British people would go to another part of the world and start to live there. That is how large parts of the east coast of America became part of the British Empire.

Discovery

Occasionally, explorers would find land and just claim it for Britain. That happened in 1770 when Captain James Cook sailed to Australia. The tribes that already lived there were ignored and Australia became part of the British Empire.

Trade

When British companies went to trade in some places, they slowly took over large areas. The government sometimes sent soldiers to help the companies. That happened in India and parts of Africa.

A long process?

As you can see, Britain got its empire in different ways. Sometimes it took over areas quickly, but often things took a lot longer. In India, for example, the British first went there to trade in the early 1600s, but it took hundreds of years before India officially became part of the British Empire.

Work

1. Test your understanding by explaining the following: empire, mother country, colony.

2. Look at **Source A**. Use the maps to describe changes in the British Empire from 1745 to 1901. Think about the number, size and location of the colonies.

3. In your own words, explain why Britain wanted an empire. You must use a quotation from **Sources B, C, D** or **E** in your answer.

4. Explain how Britain gained the following places: India, Canada, Australia, east coast of America.

7.2 What was India like before the British arrived?

At one point there were over 50 colonies in the British Empire. They were dotted all over the world and made the British Empire the largest the world had ever known. One of the largest of these 'possessions' was India. It was the colony that many Britons were most proud of, calling it the 'Jewel in the Crown' of Britain's Empire. So why were the British so keen to control India?

Mission Objectives

- Describe what India was like before the British took over.
- Examine why India was such a rich prize for a conquering nation.

Incredible India

India today is an independent country. It's the seventh largest country in the world – and the second most populated. Modern India borders Pakistan, China, Bangladesh and Nepal. India itself is a subcontinent, which means it is a huge mass of land attached to the main continent of Asia. **Source A** shows India today compared with India around 1500.

Conquest

People from all over the world have visited India, or tried to conquer it. The Persians and Iranians settled in India in ancient times. Genghis Khan invaded and looted it – and so did Alexander the Great. The Chinese came to India in pursuit of knowledge and to visit the ancient Indian universities. Then came the French… and finally the British!

SOURCE A: *India past and present.*

SOURCE B: *Brihadeeswarar Hindu Temple in Thanjavur. Hinduism originated in India.*

SOURCE C: *Mahabodhi Buddhist Temple in Bodh Gaya. Buddhism originated in India too.*

Raw materials

India is rich in natural resources – iron ore, copper, gold, silver, gemstones, spices, tea and timber. This meant that any country that made strong trade links with India could potentially become very rich and powerful… but even more rich and powerful if they managed to take over the whole country!

A divided nation?

Three of the world's major religions – Hinduism, Buddhism and Sikhism – originated in India (see **Sources B**, **C** and **D**). Other religions, such as Judaism, Christianity and Islam, have since arrived there too. At various times throughout India's history, science, technology, engineering, art, literature, mathematics, astronomy and religion have flourished there.

By the early 1500s (when many European nations began to sail to India to trade) India was divided into lots of kingdoms (see **Source A**). Most were run by Hindu princes. Occasionally the kingdoms would go to war against each other – but there were long peaceful periods too. Ruling over all the Hindu princes was the Mughal emperor. The Mughals, who were Muslims, had invaded India in the early 1500s. Within decades, the great Mughal emperor, Akbar, had managed to unite many of the Indian states (see **Source E**). He was well known for his knowledge of literature, great architecture and religious tolerance.

His grandson, Shah Jahan, who also became emperor, built the famous Taj Mahal, one of the most beautiful buildings in the world (see **Source F**). He built it in memory of his third wife – who died giving birth to their fourteenth child. However, Shah Jahan's son, Aurang Zeb, was a fanatical Muslim and picked on followers of India's other religions. As wars broke out all over India, the Mughals eventually lost control of the country. It was exactly this time (when much of India was at war) that European nations became very interested in it!

Here come the Europeans

Several European nations saw these wars in India as an opportunity to increase their own power. Many nations, but mainly the Dutch, French and British, realized that by helping certain Indian princes (with weapons and soldiers, for example), they could turn the wars any way they wanted. Then when their new ally beat the enemy, they could demand rewards from the prince – perhaps land or goods! Further, if they ever fell out with him and fought against him, they usually ended up winning… and taking his territory!

SOURCE D: *The Golden Temple in Amritsar – the holiest place of worship for Sikhs.*

SOURCE E: *Akbar the Great.*

SOURCE F: *The Taj Mahal.*

Work

1. Plan a PowerPoint® presentation called 'What was India like before the British takeover?' Include details of India's eventful history and rich culture, and explain why European nations took an interest in it. Include text and pictures. Use no more than 100 words and five slides.

7.3 Invasion of India

In 1497, a Portuguese explorer called Vasco da Gama discovered how to get to India from Europe by sea. Soon, many European countries were sending ships to India to trade. At first the ships simply reached an Indian port, swapped their goods with local traders for silk, spices, cotton or tea, and brought these home to sell for a big profit. After a few years, and with the permission of Indian rulers, the traders began to set up permanent trading stations. These were large warehouses surrounded by huge fences and guarded by men with guns (see **Source A**). So who ran the trading stations and how did they work?

Mission Objectives

- Examine how trading works.
- Discover the importance of the Battle of Plassey.

Which countries?

The British, French and Dutch were the main countries with trading stations in India in the early years, but the Danish and Portuguese traded there too (see **Source B**).

FACT!

Today, India is a single, independent country. However, when the British first started trading there, people used the word 'India' to mean the present-day countries of Pakistan, Burma (Myanmar), Bangladesh and Sri Lanka. The British gave the name 'India' to the whole lot!

The East India Company

The British trading stations in India were all run by the East India Company. Set up in 1600, it sent ships all over the world for many years. The ships left Britain full of cheap British goods, and swapped them for goods in countries as far away as Japan, China and, of course, India. Then they brought the fine china, silk, coffee and spices back to Britain to sell. The businessmen in charge of the company, and the kings and queens to whom they paid taxes, all made a fortune from this trade (see **Source C**).

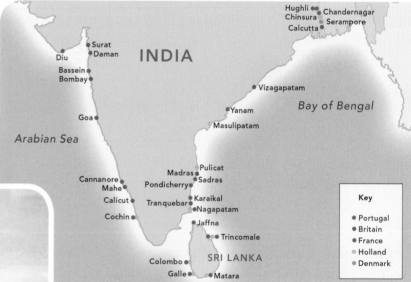

SOURCE A: *The British trading station at Bombay in 1731.*

SOURCE B: *India's trading ports – and the nations that founded them. Which continent are these nations from?*

Be a Top Historian

Top historians can spot **turning points** in history. These are points of great change, leaving things different from how they were before. In what way can the Battle of Plassey be viewed as a turning point?

SOURCE C: *How to make a fortune from trade.*

Stage 1 Get a group of rich businessmen together… and buy a ship.

Stage 2 Load the ship with goods wanted in India – guns, ammunition, swords, tools, buttons and shoes.

Stage 3 Sail to India (or perhaps China or Japan).

Stage 4 Unload the goods at the trading station – and swap them for things that are cheap and easy to get in India but hard to get in Britain!

Stage 5 Sail back to Britain with your fully loaded ship.

Stage 6 Sell the foreign goods in Britain – for far more than you paid for the British goods you swapped them for.

The fighting begins

The East India Company first set up trading posts in Surat (1612), Madras (1639) and Bombay (1668). In the 1700s, the Company began to take more Indian land. It had its own army and navy and used them against the rulers of India. At the Battle of Plassey in 1757, for example, around 3000 Company soldiers (2200 of whom were local Indians) defeated an Indian army of over 40,000 led by Prince Sirajud-Daulah. The Company fought against other European nations too – and took over their trading posts!

The Company expands

Over the following decades, various Indian rulers were either beaten in battle or played off against each other, so that more of India came under British rule. By the mid-1850s, most of India was controlled by the British… but a major rebellion that shocked the world was just around the corner!

SOURCE D: *A cigarette card showing the Company's victory at Plassey. They were led by Robert Clive (known soon after as 'Clive of India').*

Work

1 a 🖋 What is a trading station?
  b List the European countries that set up trading stations in India in the 1600s.
  c Why do you think these countries were so interested in India?

2 a What was the East India Company?
  b Explain how the Company gradually took control of most of India.
  c Why was the Battle of Plassey a significant event in Britain's takeover of India?

3 Create your own diagram, poster or leaflet explaining how the British made money from trading with India. Use **Source C** to inspire you!

7.4A Indian mutiny... or war of independence?

By the 1850s, most of India was ruled by the British. The East India Company had gradually taken more and more land and many of the British people who worked for the Company lived in great luxury in India and made huge fortunes. To help 'protect' them whilst out in India – and to make sure things ran smoothly – British soldiers were stationed all over India. The army recruited local Indians as soldiers to help them. However, on 10 May 1857, Indian soldiers (called '**Sepoys**') working for the British in Meerut (northern India) shot dead a number of British soldiers who worked with them. Soon the whole of northern India was engulfed in a ferocious fight between British and Sepoys. This is known as the Indian **Mutiny**… or the War of Independence! So what caused the uprising? How did the British respond? And why does the same event have different names?

Mission Objective

- Investigate how the events of 1857–1858 can be interpreted differently.

Suffering Sepoys

According to Queen Victoria herself, the aim of the British Empire was to 'protect the poor natives and advance civilization'. In India, the British claimed that they were *improving* India by building railways, roads, schools and hospitals.

However, in the army, the Sepoys were a very unhappy bunch. They felt that they weren't treated very well, had little hope of promotion and were often the first to be sent to the most dangerous places. Some Sepoys also felt that they were being pressured into converting to Christianity.

New guns

This build-up of anger boiled over into rebellion in 1857, when a new rifle (gun) , was delivered to the troops with a new method of loading the bullets. And it was these new bullets, and the **cartridges** that held them, that led to the start of the Empire's most bloody rebellion!

FACT!

In the 1850s, the British Army in India was made up of 200,000 Sepoys (mainly Hindus and Muslims) and 40,000 British.

SOURCE A: *Indian Sepoys in the British Army being controlled by a British Army officer.*

Load your weapons!

In January 1857, each Indian soldier was given their new rifle. The bullet (which fired from the rifle) and the gunpowder that fired it were neatly packaged together in a cartridge (see **Source B**).

Loading the cartridge was a rather complicated affair. It involved biting off the top of the cartridge, pouring the gunpowder into the gun and then ramming the rest of the cartridge (with the bullet inside) down into the gun (see **Source C**).

The problem for the Hindu and Muslim Sepoys was that the new cartridges were covered in grease to make them slide down the gun barrel easily. And because the soldier had to bite off the top of the greasy cartridge in order to get to the gunpowder, it meant that the Sepoys got grease in their mouths. And it was rumoured that the grease was made from animal fat, probably (but not definitely) a mixture of pork and beef fat – the worst possible mixture for Hindus and Muslims. After all, Hindus can't eat beef because to them a cow is sacred… and Muslims are forbidden to eat pork!

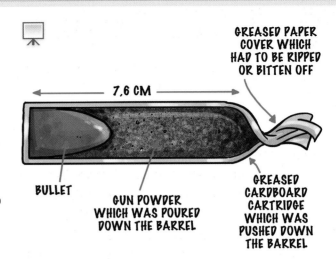

SOURCE B: *An Enfield rifle cartridge.*

GREASED PAPER COVER WHICH HAD TO BE RIPPED OR BITTEN OFF

7.6 CM

BULLET

GUN POWDER WHICH WAS POURED DOWN THE BARREL

GREASED CARDBOARD CARTRIDGE WHICH WAS PUSHED DOWN THE BARREL

Rebellion!

The Sepoys objected to the new cartridges – but were largely ignored. And when 85 Sepoys refused to use the cartridges they were arrested and sent to jail for ten years. Days later, other Sepoys rioted in support of their imprisoned comrades – and soon the whole of northern India was engulfed in rebellion.

1 Tear off the end of your cartridge (with your teeth).

2 Pour the gunpowder (which is in the cartridge) into the gun barrel.

3 Ram the cartridge (with the bullet still inside) down the barrel.

4 Take aim and FIRE!

SOURCE C: *How to load a rifle in 1857.*

Work

1 What is a Sepoy?

2 **EITHER:**
   a Copy the diagram in **Source B**. Underneath, write a short explanation of what a cartridge is.

   OR:
   b In your own words, explain how a soldier would load a rifle in the 1850s.

3 Carefully explain what caused the 1857 rebellion. You need to include what the British did in January 1857 – and why Hindu and Muslim Sepoys objected so strongly.

7.4B Indian mutiny... or war of independence?

India at war

There were major battles between British troops and Sepoys in Delhi, Cawnpore and Lucknow and both sides acted brutally. The massacre of 200 British women and children at Cawnpore, for example, outraged the British. Back home in Britain crowds bayed for blood (see **Source A**). Even Queen Victoria was horrified. Soon, 70,000 fresh troops were sent to India armed with the latest Colt revolvers made in America. And revenge was violent, bloody and swift!

When some Muslim mutineers were captured they were sewn into pig skins before they were hanged, whilst others were forced to clean up blood by licking it off the floor. One British soldier wrote of a giant tree with 130 Sepoys hanging from its branches. Especially horrible was the British punishment of being blown from the barrel of a gun (see **Source B**).

*'And England, now avenge their
    wrongs by vengeance deep and dire,*

*Cut out their cancer with the sword,
    and burn it out with fire,*

*Destroy those traitor regions,
    hang every pariah hound,*

*And hunt them down to death,
    in all hills and cities around.'*

▲ **SOURCE A:** *A British poem by Martin Tupper, written at the time of the mutiny.*

SOURCE B: *A painting showing the brutal punishment of rebel Sepoys, who have been strapped to the barrel of a gun, which will then be fired.*

FACT!

The majority of Sepoys took part in the rebellion – but not all of them. Thousands, including the Gurkhas, the Sikhs and the Pathan regiments, remained loyal to the British. Even today the Gurkhas who fight in the British Army have an astonishing reputation for loyalty to it!

The end... and after

Peace was finally declared on 8 July 1858, but the mutiny had shocked the British. For a long time it had looked as if the British might be defeated – and politicians were taken aback by the ferocity of feeling that had been shown against the British in India.

After the mutiny, the British were a lot more careful about how they governed India. They still wanted India as part of the Empire (of course), but the running of the country was taken away from the East India Company and replaced with direct rule by the British government. A new government department (the India Office) was set up and a **viceroy** was put in charge of India on behalf of Queen Victoria herself.

Before the mutiny, the British policy in India was to introduce British ideas about religion and education – which threatened the Hindu, Muslim and Sikh ways of life. After 1858, the British tried to interfere less with religious matters, and started to allow Indians more say in the running of India by allowing them jobs in local government. Even Queen Victoria commented on the new way of running India (see **Source C**). However, by 1900, nine out of ten jobs running the country were still done by Britons.

What's in a name?

Historians like to give names to different periods of time (the Ice Age, the Middle Ages, the Tudor period and so on) and to different events (the Peasants' Revolt, the English Civil War) – but no one seems to be able to agree on what to call the events of 1857–1858. At the time in Britain it was known as the 'Indian Mutiny' or the 'Sepoy Rebellion'. It is often still referred to like this in Britain today. However, for Indians and Pakistanis today, it is referred to as the 'War of Independence' or the 'Great Rebellion'. It is looked upon as the first episode in the great struggle against the British for a free India. Indeed, in 2007 the Indian and Pakistani governments celebrated the 150th anniversary of the Rebellion of 1857 with special events and ceremonies. On the official Indian government website, it is called 'The Great Rebellion' and is contained in a section entitled 'The Indian Freedom Struggle' (see **Source D**).

▶ **SOURCE D:** *A quote from the official Indian government website, india.gov.in.*

'The Hindus, Muslims and Sikhs and all other brave sons of India fought shoulder to shoulder to throw out the British'

'1857 was a pivotal point in Indian history... the better educated Indians who emerged from English-speaking schools in India, and who had learned about political parties, strikes and protest marches when they were in these schools, used these new methods against the British to gain their freedom. Had 1857 not happened, modern Indian history might have taken a quite different course.'

SOURCE E: *Based on a television interview with author William Dalrymple, September 2006.*

cartridge   mutiny
Sepoy   viceroy

'We hold ourselves bound by the same obligations of duty which bind us to our other subjects... so it is our will that our subjects of whatever race or creed, be freely and impartially admitted to offices in our service, the duties of which they may be qualified by their education, ability and integrity, duly to discharge.

▲ **SOURCE C:** *Queen Victoria's Proclamation to India, November 1858.*

Work

1 a   In what ways did the British punish the Indian rebels?

  b   Why do you think the punishments were so brutal?

2   How did the British change the way India was governed as a result of the events of 1857?

3   Look at **Source C**.

  a   What is Queen Victoria saying should happen in India?

  b   By 1901, had her wishes been carried out?

4 a   Why do you think British politicians at the time called the events of 1857 the 'Indian Mutiny'?

  b   Why do you think Indians today call the same event 'The First War of Independence'?

7.5 'The jewel in the crown'

India was the largest and richest of all the countries in Britain's Empire. In the 1850s a **viceroy**, appointed by the British in London, was put directly in charge of the country and ran it on behalf of Queen Victoria. The Queen even gave herself an extra title and started calling herself 'Empress of India' as well as 'Queen of Great Britain and Ireland'!

Mission Objective

- Identify ways that the British takeover of India could be viewed as a good thing... or a bad thing.

India was a colony that many people in Britain treasured most – even calling it 'the Jewel in the Crown'. So how did the British rule India? What was it like for Britons living there? And what was it like for Indians? Study the following sources carefully; they give a fascinating (and revealing) insight into British rule in India.

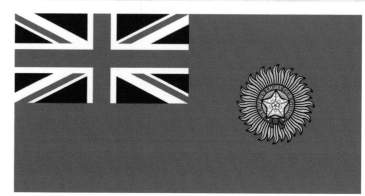

▲ **SOURCE C:** *The British India flag. The term 'British Raj' was used to describe the period of British rule in India between 1858 and 1947. The word 'raj' is Hindi for 'rule'.*

'Ceylon (now Sri Lanka) was unified under British rule in 1815. Over the next 80 years the British built 2300 miles of road and 2900 miles of railway in India. The land used for farming increased from 400,000 acres to 3.2 million acres, the schools from 170 to 2900, the hospitals from 0 to 65...'

▲ **SOURCE D:** *Written by James Morris in* Pax Britannica, *1968.*

▲ **SOURCE A:** *Many Britons abroad in India enjoyed a lifestyle far more luxurious than the one they had at home.*

'The British who lived in the colonies liked their creature comforts and were able to enjoy them more luxuriously than they generally could at home. With their hordes of servants they could live in a class above themselves.'

SOURCE B: *Written by James Morris in* Pax Britannica, *1968.*

SOURCE E: *The British built thousands of miles of railway over India. This railway station was built in Bombay (now Mumbai) in 1897. It was known as Victoria Station until 1996, when it was renamed after a seventeenth-century Hindu king.*

The Luddites

These were workers who were upset that new factory machinery could do the work ten men used to do. They formed gangs and smashed up the new machines that had cost them their jobs. They were supposedly led by Ned Ludd who lived secretly in Sherwood Forest, Nottingham – but no one ever found him!

The Swing Rioters

A few years later, the machine smashers came back. This time workers in the countryside attacked new farm machines because they were being used to do the work instead of men. Fields were set on fire, farmhouses burned and barns smashed up. They said they were led by Captain Swing – but no one ever found him either!

A meeting turns into a massacre

In August 1819, a large crowd gathered for a meeting in an area of Manchester called St Peter's Field. At this time, only a small number of men (rich ones) could vote in elections and many ordinary people (who weren't allowed to vote) thought this was unfair. So a huge meeting was planned and thousands of people attended. Whole families came, some carrying flags saying 'Votes for all'. But things got out of hand when the government sent in soldiers to stop the meeting, saying it was against the law. Soldiers on horseback, armed with swords, rode into the crowd. Eleven people were killed and over 400 injured. The youngest victim was a baby who was knocked out of his mother's arms and trampled to death by horses.

SOURCE B: *The massacre at St Peter's Field in 1819, by George Cruikshank.*

Work

1 a In your own words, explain the difference between 'revolution' and 'protest'.

b Can you think of a revolution or protest that has happened recently, in today's world?

2 a Who were the Luddites?

b What did Luddites and Swing Rioters have in common?

c How were they different?

d Why do you think Ned Ludd and Captain Swing were never caught?

3 a Why was there a meeting in St Peter's Field in August 1819?

b What happened there?

c How did the government react to the Peterloo Massacre?

FACT!

The events at St Peter's Field shocked the nation. People started to call it the **Peterloo Massacre**, a sarcastic reference to the famous Battle of Waterloo when the British defeated the French in 1815. In fact, after Peterloo, the government got even tougher on people meeting up together. New laws were introduced (known as the **Six Acts**) which banned meetings of over 50 people, tightened up gun laws and gave courts more powers to search homes and put people on trial without a jury!

Power to the people

There were lots of issues that angered ordinary people in the early 1800s – high food prices, unemployment and poor working conditions, for example. But the thing that probably angered people the most was the way Britain was ruled. Ordinary people were upset that they didn't have the right to vote… and they thought this was unfair. They felt that not being able to vote meant they couldn't do anything about their lives. So they thought that if they *could* vote in elections then the politicians who ruled the country might sort out some of the issues in their lives – like high food prices, unemployment and poor working conditions. And if they didn't, they could 'vote in' politicians who would! So what *exactly* was wrong with the way Britain was governed at this time?

SOURCE A: The Polling *by William Hogarth, 1758, a famous picture from the time showing why Britain's voting system needed to change. Can you see:*
i) *the rich men being brought in on their carriages to vote?*
ii) *one of the voters (underneath the blue flag) being told how to vote?*
iii) *two thugs dragging a sick man to the election so he can vote?*

There are around 16 million people in Britain… and only about 500,000 can vote. And they're all rich property owners!

I live in Manchester – and Manchester doesn't even have any politicians to represent us in Parliament. Nor has Birmingham or Sheffield.

I can't vote at all!

Some tiny villages have MPs. These are called 'rotten boroughs'. Appleby, a small village in Cumbria, has one voter… yet they still have an MP who goes to Parliament to help run Britain! How ridiculous is that, when huge towns like Manchester have no MPs?

And even if you have the vote, it isn't in secret. Voters are bribed to vote for people who want to become politicians.

Hungry for More?

What do you think is meant by the word 'democracy'? Discuss it as a class or write down your own definition of the word.

Change at last

By 1830, thousands of people all over Britain had been demonstrating about the voting system for many years. These people saw change (or 'reform' as it was known) as their great hope for a better life. Politicians worried that a demonstration might turn into a riot (as they often did) and that the rioters might become strong enough to take over the country by force. These MPs realized that change was needed and introduced a new system of voting (see **Source B**).

How great was the Great Reform Act?

The changes made in 1832 are often called the 'Great Reform Act' by historians. But was it so great? Still only one in five men could vote... and no women! You still had to own property to vote as well. And voting still wasn't secret – which led to the problems encountered in **Source C**.

The Great Reform Act was a huge disappointment for many ordinary working men. They wanted the vote but still didn't get it. Yes, the changes were a move in the right direction, but still four out of five men had no say in how their country was run. In 1836, a new campaign group was formed. Most members of this group simply wanted more change – but others wanted to take over the country and change it by force. The government soon saw these men as a massive threat – they were known as the **Chartists**. In 1838, they issued a list of six things they wanted (see **Source D**). The list was called the 'People's Charter', which is why the group was known as the Chartists.

The Reform Act, 1832

- More people were allowed to vote – increase in voters from 450,000 to 800,000.
- Some big towns like Manchester and Birmingham were given MPs for the first time.
- Some of the old 'rotten boroughs' were removed.

▲ **SOURCE B:** *The main points of the new voting system.*

'Everybody was told that if they voted against Colonel Anson they would be in trouble, if they voted for him they were greeted with loud cheers. If they voted for Sir Goodricke they were hissed, booed and spat on. One voter had a load of horse dung thrown all over him and dead birds were thrown at another.'

▲ **SOURCE C:** *An account of an election in Wolverhampton in 1835.*

▼ **SOURCE D:** *This is what the Chartists wanted. They discussed the possibility of including 'votes for women' but decided this was a step too far!*

Work

1. **a** Why do you think ordinary people were so keen to get the vote in the early 1800s?
   b Make a list of things that were either wrong or unfair about the voting system before 1832.
   c Look at **Source A**. Explain what is happening in the picture.

2. **a** How did the 1832 Reform Act change Britain's voting system?
   b Some people call the 1832 Reform Act a success. Others call it a failure. Why do you think there are two views about it?

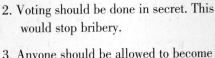

The six points of the PEOPLE'S CHARTER

1. Every man of 21 years of age or over should be allowed to vote.

2. Voting should be done in secret. This would stop bribery.

3. Anyone should be allowed to become an MP, not only those who own property.

4. MPs should be paid and then ordinary people could afford to become MPs.

5. Voting districts (constituencies) should have an equal number of voters.

6. There should be an election every year.

How did the Chartists try to change things?

Most Chartists were ordinary working people. They were shopkeepers, printers, factory workers and newsagents. They worked hard, often lived in poor housing and were always worried about high food prices, unemployment or ill health. They felt that very little was done to help them because there was no one to speak up for them in Parliament. They believed that if ordinary, working people had the vote, they could elect politicians who promised to make their lives better.

The Chartists knew that trying to get Parliament to change the voting laws was going to be difficult. So they held huge meetings, attended by thousands, in big cities such as Birmingham and Leeds to show the government that a vast number of people agreed with them. In 1839, they drew up a petition, with over one million signatures (it was nearly 5km long!) of those who supported their ideas. It was sent to Parliament so that MPs could see how many people wanted change.

Parliament rejected the petition when it arrived. So another petition was organized, this time containing three million signatures. Yet again, Parliament ignored it. Some Chartist leaders started to get angry at Parliament's refusal to listen. Some talked about taking the country over and forcing the changes. Others said this was the wrong approach and they should carry on with their peaceful petitions. Read **Sources A** and **B** carefully. Try to work out which one of the leaders wanted to use force and which one wanted to remain peaceful.

One more try

In 1848, a third petition was organized with six million signatures! The Chartists planned a huge meeting of over half a million people on Kennington Common, London, before marching to Parliament.

The government was worried – was this the start of a revolution? Plans were drawn up to defend London and Queen Victoria was moved to safety. But the meeting was a flop. It rained heavily and only around 20,000 Chartists turned up. That's right, a possible revolution failed because of bad weather!

The petition turned out to be a flop too. It was found to contain just over two million names, many of them fakes. Queen Victoria herself was supposed to have signed it ten times, as well as 'April First', 'Pug Nose', 'The Duke of Wellington' (nine times) and 'Mr Punch'! (See **Source C**). After their failure in 1848, little was heard of the Chartists again. They had failed… or had they?

> 'Let us, friends, seek to join together the honest, moral, hard-working and intelligent members of society. Let us find out about our rights from books. Let us collect information about our lives, our wages and our conditions. Then let us publish our views. Then MPs will agree there must be change, without having to use violence or arrest.'

▲ **SOURCE A:** From a speech by William Lovett, one of the Chartist leaders.

> 'I do not want to use force, but if we do not succeed we must use violence. It is better to die free men than live as slaves. Violence is the right thing to do if it wins us our freedom.'

SOURCE B: From a speech made by Feargus O'Connor, another Chartist leader.

SOURCE C: *A cartoon from* Punch *magazine showing the meeting on Kennington Common. It shows the Duke of Wellington nine times! Do you think the cartoonist is making fun of the petition?*

A success story

The Chartists were the first organized national protest movement. They drew attention to the problems of working-class people and showed that there were national issues that the government must deal with. In fact, of their six original demands, all but one (Point 6) later became law!

For a few days in the spring of 1848, the government had feared the Chartists. How close Britain came to a revolution is open for discussion but the Chartists certainly showed working people were powerful (and potentially threatening) if they came together… and that politicians should listen to them more in the future!

Power to the people

The changes to the way people voted continued after the Chartist movement. In 1867, the Second Reform Act gave the vote to every man who owned a house (which was one in three men) and, in 1884, the Third Reform Act gave even more working people the vote. In 1872, the Ballot Act said that people could vote by putting their ballot paper in a ballot box. This stopped people bribing and bullying voters into voting for them. And many more changes followed (see **Source D**).

Electoral reforms

1832	First Reform Act ('The Great Reform Act').
1858	Any man over 21 allowed to become an MP, regardless of whether they owned property or not.
1867	Second Reform Act (one man in a three could now vote).
1872	Ballot Act (voting now done in secret).
1884	Third Reform Act (two out of every three men could now vote).
1885	Voting districts (constituencies) to have equal number of voters.
1911	MPs paid.
1918	All men over 21 and many women over 30 could vote.
1928	Vote for everyone over 21.
1969	Vote for everyone over 18.

SOURCE D: *A list of reforms to Britain's voting system. Campaigns for women to be allowed to vote started in the 1860s… but it took until 1928 for all adults to get equal voting rights.*

What Happened When?

1848 is sometimes known as the 'Year of Revolution' because there were so many protests, revolutions and attempted revolutions across Europe. Why not find out about events in 1848 in Italy, France, Austria, Hungary or Belgium, for example?

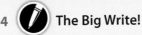

Work

1. **a** Who were the Chartists? (See p.129).
   b List their six demands.
   c Pick two that you think were most important to the workers. Give reasons for your choices.
   d Which of the six demands is not in force today?
   e Can you think why this has never been made a law?

2. Why were the following unsuccessful?
   - The Kennington Common meeting
   - The Chartists' third petition

3. Look at **Sources A** and **B**.
   a Rewrite each source in your own words.
   b Write a sentence to explain these two words:
   - reformer - revolutionary
   c In your opinion, who was the reformer and who was the revolutionary? Give reasons for your decision.

4. **The Big Write!**

   Choose **one** of the following to complete.
   EITHER:
   a Write an essay that answers the question, 'Were the Chartists a success or not?' Organize your essay into short paragraphs:
   - What changes did the Chartists want?
   - Why did working people join them?
   - How did they try to get change?
   - What had they achieved by 1850?
   - Were they a long-term success, or a short-term one?

   OR:
   b Imagine it is 1848 and you work for the government. Your job is to write a report explaining who the Chartists are, what they want and why they are attracting so much support.

The match girls

Different people have different opinions about the same sorts of things. For example, you might like a pop group that your friends can't stand or love a TV programme or film that your parents don't like. Sometimes two people can watch the *same* event, like a football match, and have completely different views about it. If Manchester United, for example, played Liverpool and lost one-nil, the Manchester fan would have a very different opinion about the game than a Liverpool supporter! This difference of opinion about the same thing happens a lot in History – and top historians should be able to spot when it is happening and try to work out why. Look at the four characters below and read about them. Then, you're going to study an event that took place in 1888 and try to imagine what each of the characters might feel about this same event.

Mission Objectives

- Investigate the Match Girls Strike of 1888.
- Propose how different people might react to it.

Who were the match girls?

Match girls produced matches that were used to light things like fires and cigars. In the 1800s, one of the largest producers of matches was the Bryant & May factory in the East End of London. On a match at that time, the bit that burst into flame was made from white **phosphorus**, which is an explosive chemical… and poisonous! The fumes from white phosphorus can attack the teeth and even cause death. Teeth can rot and drop out after a few months. The disease could spread to the jawbone too and rot it away. Sometimes an infected person's jaw had to be completely removed.

More side effects

About 1400 match girls worked in the Bryant & May factory and many had nasty skin diseases. The factory didn't have sinks for workers to wash their hands so the phosphorus burnt their skin and got into the food they ate. Some workers lost their hair and others shone in the dark because phosphorus is luminous. And they only earned a measly weekly wage of 20p (for a girl) or 40p (for a woman), much of which went on silly fines.

White slaves

In 1888, a campaigner and journalist, Annie Besant, interviewed some of the women. She published what she found out in an article called 'White Slavery in London'. As you'd expect, the factory owners weren't happy. They sacked the women who spoke to Besant and forced the others to sign a document saying that the conditions in the factory were good. One woman who refused to sign was sacked.

A match girl, who worked in the Bryant and May factory.

A dockworker who worked on London's docks loading and unloading ships.

A politician.

Mr William Bryant, one of the owners of the Bryant & May Match Company.

▶ **SOURCE A:** *A photograph of Annie Besant, taken in 1889. Besant supported a number of workers' demonstrations for better working conditions, campaigned for better women's rights and supported the idea of India, one of Britain's colonies, being allowed to rule itself!*

A strike

Besant helped the workers to organize a strike. She also held public meetings and raised money to give to the striking women. Many newspapers took the side of the women and within two weeks the women had been promised better pay, better conditions and an end to the petty fines… so they went back to work.

More strikes

Later that year, the London dockworkers, who earned even less than the match girls, went on strike. And after a long and bitter strike, they got a pay rise too!

SOURCE C: *Match girls (and a boy) on strike in 1888. Besant got them lots of publicity and told them to walk around the West End of London (a richer area).*

SOURCE D: *A drawing of matchmakers in 1871.*

Be a Top Historian

Top historians realize that different people tell different stories about the past… and a person's version of their story is influenced by their own attitudes and beliefs at the time of constructing their view. These personal viewpoints or opinions are known as **interpretations**.

Wise Up Words

phosphorus

'In less than a fortnight, the girls were promised better conditions. The fines were ended and box-fillers given a nine per cent pay rise. It was a milestone in union history and other victories soon followed. In 1889, the gas workers demanded – and got – an eight-hour day. Later that year, the London dockers went on strike… they also won.'

SOURCE B: *Written by modern historian J F Aylett in 1991.*

Work

1   a   What is white phosphorus?
    b   Describe the effects of white phosphorus poisoning.
2   a   How did Annie Besant help the match girls?
    b   Why do you think Besant used the title 'White Slavery in London' for her article about the match girls?
    c   Can you suggest why it was hard for unskilled workers, like the match girls, to go on strike?

3   Look at the four characters on page 132. For each one, write down one or two things that they might feel about:
    • the Bryant and May Factory
    • Annie Besant
    • the results of the match girl strike.

4   Design a campaign poster in support of the striking match girls. Include as many facts about the factory conditions as you can, and what needs to be done. Include one or two striking images, and a headline.

Enough of history... what about herstory?

In 1832, Joseph Thomson tried to sell his wife at auction for 50 shillings (£2.50). Look at **Source A** to discover what he told buyers. Unbelievably, Mr Thomson managed to sell his wife for 20 shillings (£1.00) and a dog! Today, we are shocked by the actions of this man. In fact, what Mr Thomson did is now against the law, but in 1832, it wasn't. Mr Thomson was simply treating his wife as his property – and he was free to do whatever he wanted with her. Look through **Sources B** to **F** carefully. In today's world where men and women have equal rights under the law, it is difficult to imagine women's place in society at that time.

Mission Objectives

- Assess the position of women in the eighteenth and nineteenth centuries.
- Analyse a variety of sources relating to the position of women.

'Gentlemen, I offer my wife, Mary Anne Thomson, whom I mean to sell to the highest bidder. It is her wish as well as mine to part forever. She has been a snake to me. I took her for my comfort but she has turned into a curse, a tormentor and a daily devil. However, she has a bright and sunny side. She can read novels, milk cows, make butter and shout at our maid. She cannot make rum, gin or whisky, but she is a good judge from long experience in tasting them.'

▲ **SOURCE A:** *Joseph Thomson speaking at an auction in 1832.*

'[In 1800], once married, her husband owned her… that was the law of the land. A wife's duty was to obey her husband. If she did not, he could beat her. A wife's duty was to please her husband; if she did not he might take a mistress. Either way, there was almost nothing she could do about it. An Act of Parliament was necessary to end a marriage. It could cost £2000 and only two women ever did it. It was quite different for the man. He could spend all "her" money and she could not stop him. If he got into debt, her possessions could be taken to pay off the debts… even her clothes!'

▲ **SOURCE B:** *From J F Aylett's* The Suffragettes and After.

'In every way, both mental and physical, the average woman is **inferior** to the average man.'

▲ **SOURCE C:** *Adapted from an essay by Thomas Huxley, a leading scientist in the 1800s.*

'An exquisite slave, a humble, flattering, smiling, child-loving, tea-making, piano-playing being who laughs at all our jokes, however old they are, helps us and fondly lies to us throughout life.'

▲ **SOURCE D:** *The writer W M Thackeray's views on how many men viewed women at this time. Make sure you understand words such as 'exquisite', humble and 'fondly'.*

SOURCE E: *A punishment for nagging wives in 1812, the **Ducking Stool**.*

Thomas Barnardo

Thomas Barnardo set up a school for the poor in London in 1867. He opened his first home for poor children in 1870. One evening, an 11-year-old boy named John Somers (nicknamed 'Carrots') was turned away because the home was full. He was found two days later, dead from the cold. From then on, Barnardo promised never to turn away another child from his home. He had to open more and more to cope with the vast number of destitute children. By the time of his death in 1905, Barnardo's homes had rescued over 50,000 homeless, orphaned and crippled boys and girls. Barnardo's is still Britain's largest children's charity at present.

Believe in children
Barnardo's

SOURCE E: *The Barnardo's logo today.*

SOURCE F: *Thomas Barnardo.*

Who else?

These philanthropists were not alone. Others, like William Wilberforce, Angela Burdett-Coutts, Titus Salt, Octavia Hill and Joseph Rowntree, worked just as hard to end slavery, improve education, and improve working and living conditions. Often wealthy themselves, they thought it their moral duty to draw attention to those living the most miserable lives of all and make the government aware that it was its job to protect and help those people.

Philanthropy today

Today, we like to think we live in a caring society. We don't tolerate abuse, cruelty, bullying or appalling living and working conditions. We are all proud of the money we raise to help people less fortunate than ourselves by taking part in sponsored walks or swims and events like Children in Need and Comic Relief. In many ways, we are carrying on the work of the great philanthropists of the nineteenth century!

FACT!

The government *did* try to help the poorest of the poor – but its help didn't always make life better. A law in 1834 said that those fit enough to work, but who didn't have a job, had to go into a **workhouse**. This was a grim, large building in each town where the poor were kept like prisoners. They were forced to work, families were separated, uniforms were worn and rules were harsh. The thought of going 'into the workhouse' haunted every person in the 1800s!

Hungry for More?

Why not research the life and work of one of the great philanthropists – perhaps Joseph Rowntree, Titus Salt or Angela Burdett-Coutts (who was known as 'the richest woman in Britain')? Alternatively, research one of the famous charitable organizations set up at the time. There are lots to choose from – Royal National Institute of Blind People (1868), St John Ambulance (1877), RSPB (1889), Action for Children (1869), Children's Society (1881), RSPCA (1824), British Red Cross (1870), Blue Cross (1897).

Work

1 a What is a philanthropist?
  b Write no more than two sentences about each of the following: Benjamin Waugh, William Booth, Thomas Barnardo.
  One sentence must outline their achievements, whilst the other must mention an interesting fact.

  TOP TIP: *Plan your sentences in rough first.*

2 Look at **Source C**.
  a In your own words, explain what Booth meant.
  b Why do you think he uses the words 'I'll fight' so often?

3 a What was a workhouse?
  b Why do you think the poor feared them?

4 a What 'charitable' work have you done? Give examples.
  b Can you think of any modern philanthropists?

What were Victorian schools like?

During the Victorian era, there were many investigations that looked at the way people lived and worked. Many of the investigators asked children for their opinions. As a result, we have a good view of what life was like during this time. In 1841, a group of boys told a government enquiry that they'd never heard of London and thought the Queen's name was Albert. Few had heard of Jesus Christ either – 'Does 'e work down our pit?' asked one young miner. And these boys were being serious. They could not read or write or do simple sums. Something had to change.

Time for school

By the early 1800s, some people started to think children should be taught at least some basic skills. For this they needed to go to proper schools.

By the 1850s, about six children in ten were getting some teaching but the quality was not very good! Some youngsters went to a **dame school** for an hour or more a week. Run by a local woman in her front room, a child might learn to count and say the alphabet in return for a few pennies. If this was too expensive (and for many it was), parents could send their children to a **ragged school**. First set up in 1844 for orphans and very poor children, these places often had 300 students in one room with one proper teacher! 'Pupil teachers' (older boys) took lots of the lessons and, needless to say, very little learning was done. Many children stayed away from school altogether. They were far too busy earning money in factories!

By the late 1860s, the government saw that Britain needed more educated people. Engineers and scientists were needed to build and design machines. They had to understand mathematics. Mechanics needed to read instruction manuals and secretaries and clerks needed to know how to write letters and calculate prices. Even factory workers had to be able to read notices! So in 1870, the government introduced the Elementary Education Act. This said:

- A school should be built in any area where there isn't one, paid for by local taxes.

- There should be a school place for every child in the area aged five to twelve.
- Parents had to pay a small fee, but it was free for the very poor.
- The schools could force some youngsters to attend, but school wasn't compulsory!

Ten years later, in 1880, education from five to ten was made compulsory… and in 1891 it became free! So what was the new school system like?

What was the timetable like?

Education was designed to equip children for life after school. There was some PE, known as 'drill', and some History and Geography too.

SCHOOL TIMETABLE

Boys

Morning (9:00am–12 noon)

The three Rs = Reading, Writing and Arithmetic (done together with girls)

Afternoon (2:00pm–5:00pm)

Science, Woodwork and Technical Drawing

Girls

Morning (9:00am–12 noon)

The three Rs = Reading, Writing and Arithmetic (done together with boys)

Afternoon (2:00pm–5:00pm)

Cookery, Needlework and Housework

SOURCE A: *This timetable is from a typical day at school in Bristol in 1897. Why do you think the girls and the boys learned different things?*

Before you dream of inventing a time machine to take you back before 1870 so you won't have to go to school, don't think you'd spend your days playing out with friends or lying in bed! If you were an ordinary child living before 1870, there'd be one thing you'd be doing all day – working (probably down a mine or in a factory six days a week)!

SOURCE B: *A photograph of a Victorian schoolroom. Can you see one of the students asleep on the front row?*

What did the schoolroom look like?

Students sat at wooden desks in rows, facing a blackboard and a large world map. Some had walked miles to get to the cold, draughty schoolroom.

Wise Up Words

dame school   logbook   ragged school   tutor

Work

1 **a** What was:
   i a dame school?
   ii a ragged school?
   b According to the government, why were these schools not good enough to educate Britain's children?

2 Look at **Source A**.
   a What were the 'three Rs'?
   b Do you think this is a sensible name for these three subjects? Explain your answer.

   c Why do you think boys and girls were taught different things in the afternoon?

3 Look at **Source B**.
   a Make a list of some of the major differences between the classroom in **Source B** and the one you are sitting in.
   b What is the biggest difference?

SOURCE A: *A lesson in housework, 1893.*

What were the lessons really like?

Lessons must have been pretty boring! Students copied from the blackboard or repeated things as a whole group. In Geography, they might list all the countries on the globe or learn all the names of the railway stations between London and Crewe. **Source A** shows girls learning how to do housework correctly – the boys would never have learned this.

How did schools keep records?

Every school had a **logbook**. It recorded everything that happened on a day-to-day basis. Carefully read the true events from Milton House School logbook (**Source B**) and prepare to be amazed…

> **Hungry for More?**
>
> Why do you think that boys and girls have the same range of subjects to learn today?

4 September 1879
   Mr Brown was reported to have punished a boy by striking him over the head with a stick. After school had ended, Mrs Barnes called with her daughter Catherine to show an injury that Mr Brown had done to her arm by hitting her on the elbow with a stick. Mr Brown expressed deep regret and promised that such a thing should not happen again.

8 April 1881
   One death during the week from fever. Every member of the Craig family ill with fever and in hospital.

6 May 1881
   Margaret Luke (Class 6) died on Monday.

13 May 1881
   Lots of truants. Parents told to come to school tomorrow.

25 November 1881
   Sent for Mrs Ferguson. Ordered her to take home her daughter and clean her head, which is overrun with lice. This has not been noticed until now as she had a bandage over her head.

25 December 1881
   School as normal.

SOURCE B: *Milton House Public School's logbook.*

What about naughty children?

Teachers were tough – and so were punishments. Being rude, leaving school without permission, sulking, answering back, throwing ink and being late were all punishable offences (see **Source C**).

What equipment did they use?

Younger children learned to write on slates, using slate pencils. Paper was expensive but slate could be used again and again. The students just rubbed out the letters when they'd finished. Older students used paper 'copybooks' and wrote in them with a metal-nibbed wooden pen. They dipped their nibs into ink-pots and scratched the letters onto the page. They had to be careful not to spill any ink!

Be a Top Historian

Top historians can **analyse** sources and **extract** the correct information to answer a particular question. Sometimes you'll have to use a number of different sources to help your investigation.

FACT!

Rich boys were taught at home by private **tutors** until they were seven or eight years old. Then they went away to expensive boarding schools to learn Latin, Greek, Literature, History, Geography, Science and Sport. Rich girls stayed at home. They learned to sew, look after a home, cook, sing and play musical instruments.

SOURCE C: *These punishments were all used in British schools. Hitting students, usually over the hand or bottom, with a cane, ruler or slipper was eventually banned by the government in 1986.*

Work

1 Look at **Source B**.
   a What is a logbook?
   b Why was Mr Brown in trouble?
   c Why was Mrs Ferguson asked to come into school?
   d Does anything surprise you about the last entry in the logbook?

2 Look at **Source C**.
   a Why do you think schools had these punishments?
   b Which of these punishments do you think is the most cruel? Give reasons for your answer.
   c Why do you think the government eventually banned these punishments in British schools?
   d Should any of these punishments be re-introduced? Give reasons for your answer.

3 Imagine you are a student at the sort of Victorian school described on these pages. You have been asked to prepare an 'induction leaflet' that will be given to all new students starting at the school (you may have been given something similar yourself!). Write your leaflet, remembering to include:
   - information about the lessons they'll be doing
   - methods of teaching and learning
   - a description of a typical schoolroom
   - some of the rules in place and what to expect if rules are broken.
   - a guide to the equipment in use.

Look at **Source A**. It is a painting from around 1745. The patient is in absolute agony. Look at his face; he is being held down while the surgeon cuts off his leg. The poor man won't have been given any painkilling drugs – he is completely awake when the surgeon starts to slice into his skin and saw through his thighbone. It is highly unlikely that the medical equipment being used has ever been washed either. It will be stained with the dry blood and pus from a previous patient. One well-known surgeon used to sharpen his knives on the sole of his boot before using them. And you know how filthy the streets were! What do you think patients' chances of survival were? Why were conditions so bad? And why have they improved so much since then?

Mission Objectives

- Outline how and why attitudes towards cleanliness changed in the nineteenth century.
- Explain how surgeons won the battle against pain and infection.
- Assess the significance of important surgeons.

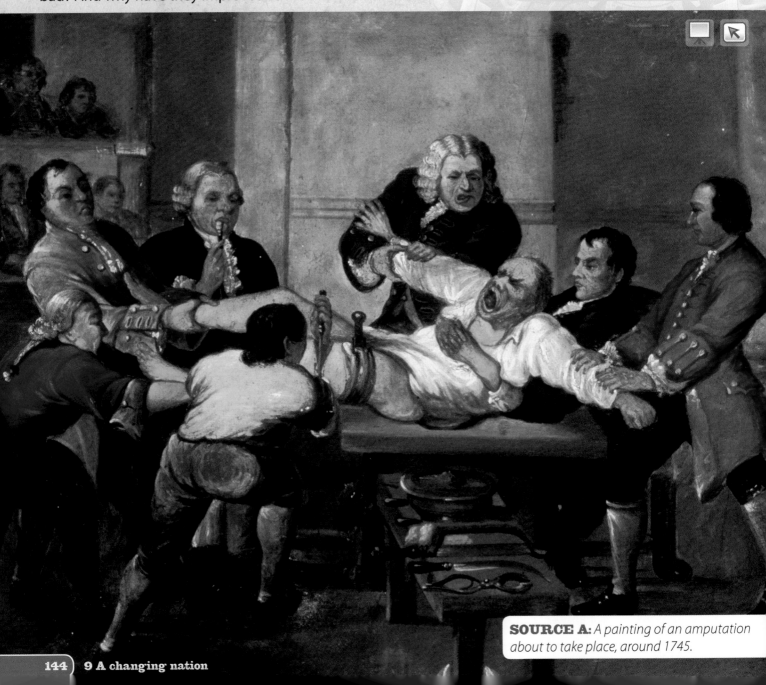

SOURCE A: *A painting of an amputation about to take place, around 1745.*

The enemy within

In 1745, a patient in a British hospital had two major enemies. One was the pain during the operation; the other was infection afterwards. Either could kill you! Only when these two obstacles were dealt with would it be possible to make any real medical progress. In the nineteenth century, doctors started to find the solutions to these problems… and changed the way the sick were cared for forever!

Can I have something for the pain?

For hundreds of years, doctors and surgeons had tried to reduce a patient's pain during surgery. Getting them drunk or knocking them out were two of the most common methods. But, in 1846, an American dentist called William Morton tried out a new idea. He put his patients to sleep for a short period of time using a gas called **ether**. It worked! The patient felt no pain during the operation, woke up 20 minutes later and went home. Anaesthetics (based on the word 'ether') were born and the idea soon caught on among London's surgeons. However, ether irritated patients' eyes and made them cough and vomit during operations. So, in 1847, a Scottish doctor called James Simpson tried **chloroform** as an alternative. Again, it worked, but had fewer of the nasty side effects of ether. Soon, chloroform became the most common anaesthetic in the land – even Queen Victoria used it in 1853 as a painkiller while giving birth to her son Leopold.

Horrible hospitals

The use of anaesthetic was a great step forward but it didn't stop people dying from infections after operations. Hospitals were dirty places, where patients were all herded together whether they had a highly contagious fever or a broken arm. The operating theatres were no better. The only thing that was ever cleaned out was the sand box from under the operating table, which was used to catch a patient's blood during surgery. Doctors and surgeons didn't understand the need for cleanliness because they didn't know that germs caused disease. It would take a few more famous men to solve this problem!

FACT!

In the 1840s, a famous London surgeon named Robert Liston held the world record for **amputating** a leg – two and a half minutes. Unfortunately, he worked so fast that he accidentally cut off the patient's testicles! Also, he once slashed a spectator's coat during another operation and the spectator dropped dead with fright.

Be a Top Historian

Top historians know **how** and **why** changes take place. Some key changes happen as a result of **turning points**. These are times of great change or important events or discoveries that leave things permanently different from how they were before. What were the turning points in the fight against pain and infection?

FACT!

The word 'hospital' comes from the Latin word 'hospitale', meaning 'a place for guests'. By 1745, London had some of the finest hospitals in Europe. St Bartholomew's was the oldest but, by this time, rich men with a desire to do good things had donated money to help open many others. Westminster, Guy's, St George's Infirmary and Middlesex hospitals were all built before 1745 and, even today, still provide medical care for Britain's citizens.

Work

1 Write a short description of the scene in **Source A**. Use no more than 100 words.

2 Make a list of things in **Source A** that would not happen during an operation today.

3 In your own words, using names and dates, explain how the problem of pain during operations was dealt with in the 1800s.

The fight against infection

By the end of the 1850s, surgeons were able to perform much better operations. They could spend longer working on the patients because they were 'under anaesthetic' and there was no danger of them waking up and dying of pain and shock. However, people still continued to die of blood poisoning and nasty infections because surgeons did not understand the importance of keeping things clean! They just didn't realize the danger of dirt! Read **Source A** carefully.

> 'A strong, young farmer came into the hospital and told the surgeon that his girlfriend had made comments about his nose – it was too much to one side; could it be straightened? He had heard of the wonderful things that were done in London hospitals. He was admitted; the septum (bone between the nostrils) was straightened and in five days he was dead. He died of hospital sepsis.'

SOURCE A: *Visiting a hospital was a risky business (adapted from J Leeson in* Lister as I Knew Him, *1927).*

Germ warfare

'Sepsis' is the Greek word for 'rotten'. The farmer's wound had gone rotten and he had died from blood poisoning (**Source A**). In fact, the number of patients dying after operations in the 1850s was astonishing – as many as six out of ten! Then, in the 1860s, a French scientist named Louis Pasteur made a major breakthrough. He discovered that germs (such as bacteria) caused disease... and he changed medical understanding forever! He went on to say that many of these germs could be killed by heat – and proved it in his laboratory. We still use **pasteurization** – the heating of food and drink (check your milk carton!) – to help prevent infection today.

Acid attack

In 1865, a British doctor, Joseph Lister, took Pasteur's theories one step further. He thought that it might be germs that caused so many of his patients to die from sepsis. Surely, he believed, if the germs were killed with antiseptic ('anti' means against), then more of his patients would survive. Lister chose carbolic acid as his antiseptic. Using a pump, a bit like an aerosol can,

he sprayed anything that might possibly come into contact with the wound. Spray everything, he hoped, and all the germs would die. He was right! His patient didn't get any infections and antiseptics were born (see **Source B**).

Soon doctors and surgeons all over the country were trying antiseptic sprays and other cleaner ways to work. Hospitals waged a war against germs. Walls were scrubbed clean, floors were swept and equipment was **sterilized**. Surgeons started to wear rubber gloves, surgical gowns and face masks during operations (see **Source C**).

FACT!

Some people called Lister a miracle worker. Perhaps you can see why! According to figures from Newcastle Infirmary in 1878, before Lister's antiseptic invention was widely used, out of every ten people:

Six died and four lived (after a major operation).

After Lister's widespread use of antiseptic:

One died and nine lived (after a major operation).

SOURCE B: *Antiseptic in action. An operation using Lister's carbolic acid spray. Note the doctor on the left putting the patient 'to sleep' with an anaesthetic.*

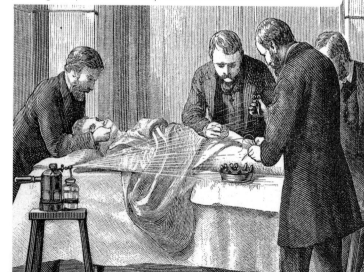

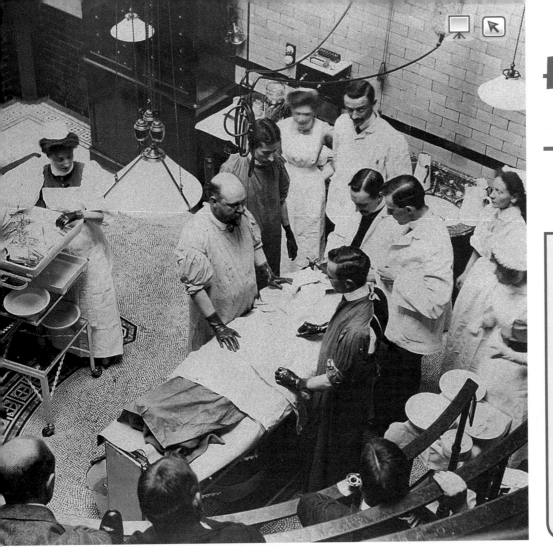

Wise Up Words

pasteurization   sepsis
sterilize   vaccination

Hungry for More?

Florence Nightingale is one of the most famous nurses in the world. She lived from 1820 to 1910. Find out:
• why she is so famous
• how she changed nursing forever
• why she is called 'the lady with the lamp'.
Use the Internet, or your school or local library.

SOURCE C: *An operation in 1901. Look for all the different ways in which this surgeon tries to keep a cleaner operating room.*

FACT!

For years, Edward Jenner had observed that people with cowpox (a mild and harmless disease) didn't get smallpox (a serious killer disease). So, in 1796, he took pus from the blister of a girl who had cowpox and squirted it into two cuts in the arm of an eight-year-old boy named James Phipps. Next he injected Phipps with smallpox. It was a risky experiment but the boy didn't catch the deadly disease! Jenner had discovered a way of preventing smallpox, one of Britain's biggest killers. Soon doctors were calling this method **vaccination**, from 'vacca', the Latin word for 'cow'. By the 1880s, it was widely accepted that one way to prevent disease was to inject a weakened form of the germ in order to allow the body to build up its own defences. This is how it is done today.

Work

1   Write a sentence or two to explain the following words:
     • sepsis • pasteurization • sterilize • vaccination

2 a In your own words, explain how Jenner, Pasteur and Lister improved people's health. Make sure you include key words like 'germs', 'vaccination' and 'antiseptic' in your answer.

  b Was one of these men more important than the other or were they equally important? Give reasons for your answer.

3   Look at **Source A** on page 145 and **Source C** above.

  a Draw two spider diagrams, one describing the main features of an operation in 1745 and the other describing the main features in 1901.

  b Compare the two diagrams and write a paragraph explaining how operations had changed between 1745 and 1901.

  c Look at your 1901 diagram and think about a modern operation. Circle the things that have changed since 1901 in one colour and underline the things that still happen today in another.

For some of you, it is probably hard to imagine a trip to the shops without coming back with some sort of chocolate treat. In fact, Britain regularly appears in the list of the top ten chocolate-eating countries, with each UK citizen eating over 7kg of chocolate per year (on average). To put it another way, that means all of us eat around 157 chocolate bars a year. The chocolate industry is a multi-million pound business and Britain's largest chocolate maker is a company called Cadbury. So how did this world-famous company start? How did it become one of the most recognized brands in history? And what does the Cadbury story tell us about life, work and business in Victorian Britain?

Mission Objectives

- Understand the origins of drinking and eating chocolate in Britain.
- Explain the aims and motives of the Cadbury family in relation to their world-famous chocolate company.

Chocolatl

It was the ancient Mayan and Aztec peoples of Central America who first enjoyed a drink called 'chocolatl'. It was a much-prized spicy drink made from roasted and ground-up cacao beans (harvested from the pods of cacao trees), mixed with water and spices. Cacao beans were so valuable that they were sometimes used as currency. An early explorer in Central America found that ten beans could buy him a rabbit, while 100 beans could buy him a slave!

Chocolate spreads

Spanish explorers were the first to bring 'chocolatl' back to Europe in the early 1500s. Soon, 'chocolate' became one of Spain's most fashionable (and expensive) drinks and, over the next 150 years, it spread to Italy (in 1606), France (1615), Germany (1646) and then Britain (1650s), where it was enjoyed by King Charles II. By then, sugar was being added instead of some of the spices and it was discovered that chocolate tasted even better hot!

Chocolate houses

High taxes on cacao beans meant that chocolate was only a drink for the wealthy. In 1657, Britain's first 'Chocolate House' was opened by a Frenchman in London, where the rich could go for a glass of wine, a gossip, a mug of beer… and a cup of hot drinking chocolate (see **Sources B**, **C** and **D**). Around 1700, some chocolate houses started to add milk to improve the taste further.

SOURCE A: *Aztecs making 'chocolatl' in the 1600s. Here they are roasting, then crushing, the cocoa beans before adding water to the spices.*

SOURCE B: *A 'Chocolate House' in London, 1733.*

'In Bishopgate Street, in Queen's Head Alley, at a Frenchman's house, is an excellent West Indian drink called chocolate, to be sold, where you may have it ready at any time, and also at reasonable prices.'

▲ **SOURCE C:** *Britain's first ever advert for chocolate, in 1657.*

'Went to Mr Bland's and there drank my morning draft of chocolate.'

SOURCE D: *Written by the famous diarist Samuel Pepys.*

Here comes Cadbury

In 1824, John Cadbury opened a shop in the centre of Birmingham selling tea and coffee. He also introduced a new product to sell – drinking chocolate. As a Quaker he felt that these were a better alternative to alcohol – which he believed was a cause of misery among working people at the time. Soon, Cadbury was selling 16 different types of drinking chocolate. He even sold solid cocoa blocks, which customers could take home, scrape a little off and mix it with sugar and hot milk. He opened his first small factory making his different types of drinking chocolate in the centre of Birmingham in 1831.

Chocolate for eating

No one knows who first produced chocolate just for eating but in 1847 a company called J S Fry and Sons from Bristol sold a 'delicious chocolate to eat'. Two years later, John Cadbury's shop sold a similar product. The 'eating chocolate' available at this time would have been nowhere near as nice as the chocolate we enjoy today. Despite this, business was so good that the Cadbury company moved to a larger factory. By 1854, he had even sold some of his drinking chocolate to Queen Victoria. John Cadbury retired in 1861 and handed over the business to his sons, George and Richard.

FACT!

The Cadbury family were Quakers. Quakers were well known for campaigning for justice, equality and an end to poverty. Many Quakers made their mark on British business, including the Fry family from Bristol, the Rowntree and Terry families from York (who both made sweets) and Sampson Lloyd from Birmingham, who founded Lloyds Bank.

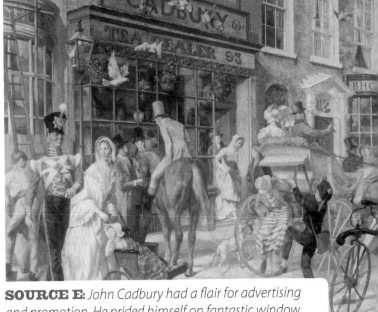

SOURCE E: *John Cadbury had a flair for advertising and promotion. He prided himself on fantastic window displays – and a Chinese man, in full national costume, working behind the counter!*

Work

1 Explain each of these words:
• chocolatl • chocolate houses • Quakers.

2 What role did each of these play in making chocolate popular?
  i   Spanish explorers   iii John Cadbury
  ii Chocolate houses   iv   J S Fry.

SOURCE F:
An early advert for Fry's eating chocolate. Fry and Sons merged with Cadbury Brothers in 1919.

The Cadbury brothers

In 1866, George visited a factory in Holland and brought back new ideas for making top quality chocolate. By the 1870s, the brothers' new techniques meant that sales of drinking and eating chocolate were going up.

A new type of factory

In 1879, the Cadbury Brothers, as the company was now known, moved into a state-of-the-art factory, 6km south of the centre of Birmingham, known as Bournville. Absolutely everything – product design, chocolate making, packaging, advertising – was done in the same place. By 1899, the Bournville factory had trebled in size and employed nearly 3000 people. However, a 'Cadbury worker' led a different kind of life to employees in some of Britain's factories!

Cadbury cares

The Cadbury brothers believed passionately in improving the lives of their workers. Around the factory, they built a 'model village' of 300 houses – for their workers. They were light and comfortable with large gardens. They even built a swimming pool, a bowling green, football, cricket and hockey pitches, and tennis and squash courts. However, there were no pubs because they didn't want to encourage their workers to drink. To fill their employees' leisure time, outings were organized and the firm was amongst the first to introduce a half-day holiday on a Saturday and adopt the custom of closing the factory on bank holidays. 'Workers' councils' were also set up, with the role of discussing health, safety, rewards, training, social life and working conditions.

Richard died in 1899 but George kept going for many years. Even in his seventies he used to cycle into Birmingham to teach working men to read and write, and give Bible classes. He even used to eat breakfast in the factory canteen with his workers each morning.

'Why should industrial areas be dirty and depressing? Why shouldn't the industrial worker enjoy country air and occupations without being separated from his work? And if the country is a good place to live in, why not to work in?'

SOURCE C: The thoughts of George Cadbury.

▲ **SOURCE A:** The famous Bournville factory surrounded by its sports and leisure facilities and workers' housing. George Cadbury called it the 'factory in a garden'. It was an ideal spot to build a factory too – close to a canal, good roads, a railway and water supply.

▲ **SOURCE B:** Houses in Bournville, near Birmingham, 1905.

▲ **SOURCE D:** A Dairy Milk advert from 1928. Three names were considered in total: Jersey, Highland Milk and Dairy Maid, which was chosen but then changed to Dairy Milk a few weeks before going on sale.

▲ **SOURCE E:** George Cadbury, 1839–1922.

A world-famous chocolate bar

Cadbury first added milk to eating chocolate in 1897. It wasn't the first to do it (the French and Swiss had done it for years) but its 'milk chocolate' proved to be a big seller. In 1901, the company decided to produce a new milk chocolate bar to rival the other milk chocolate from abroad. In 1905, what was to become Cadbury's top selling brand – Dairy Milk – was launched and took the chocolate world by storm. Today, more than 250 million bars of Cadbury's Dairy Milk are made every year; that's enough bars to cover 92 football pitches five times over. And the secret recipe is still kept under lock and key in a safe under the Bournville factory in Birmingham. Other chocolate products soon followed (see **Source F**).

The Cadbury legacy

George Cadbury died in 1922 – but lived to see the company he helped make famous become Britain's biggest chocolate maker. By the time of his death, he employed nearly 8000 workers, some of whom lived in some of Britain's best working-class housing with excellent facilities. The Bournville Estate continued to grow and today covers over 405 hectacres. Over 100 years later, the company still gives support to community projects such as special-needs housing for the elderly, children in care and people with learning difficulties. And true to the Cadbury family's beliefs, there are still no pubs in the Bournville area!

▼ **SOURCE F:** *A timeline showing the development of Cadbury from 1905.*

1905	Dairy Milk
1915	Milk Tray
1919	Cadbury merges with J S Fry and Sons, Britain's biggest chocolate seller of the 1800s. Cadbury keeps the Fry name for some of its products, though.
1920	Flake
1928	Fruit and Nut
1929	Crunchie
1933	Whole Nut
1938	Cadbury's Roses launched. Today, over 1300 million Roses chocolates are sold every year in the UK – enough for more than 20 per person!
1948	Fudge
1958	Picnic
1960	Buttons
1970	Curly Wurly
1971	Creme Egg
1976	Double Decker
1983	Wispa
1985	Boost
1987	Twirl
1989	Cadbury buys Trebor and Bassett sweet companies
1989	White Buttons, Chomp
1992	Timeout
1999	Heroes and Giant Buttons

Work

1 Each of these dates is important in the history of Cadbury:
   - 1824   • 1831   • 1849   • 1854   • 1861
   - 1866   • 1879   • 1897   • 1899   • 1905   • 1922

   In your workbook, write each date on a separate line and next to each one, write down what happened in that year.

2 a Explain how each of the following factors helped Cadbury develop:
   i new technology
   ii religious beliefs
   iii good business sense
   iv fashionable nature of chocolate products
   v treatment of workers.

   b Do you think one factor is more important than the others, or do you think each factor contributed equally? Explain your answer carefully.

3 a Describe Cadbury's Bournville factory and village.
   b In what ways were the Bournville factory and village different to other factories and towns that you have studied?
   c Why do you think Cadbury created the Bournville factory and village in this way?

4 It is 1905 and Cadbury's newest chocolate bar, 'Dairy Milk', is just about to go on sale. The company has spent years developing it and hopes it will become the most popular chocolate bar in the world… and it wants you to design a poster to advertise it. So, what slogan will you use? What will you say about the bar itself? How will you describe it? Will you mention how it is made and the origins of the product? What pictures will you use? Make sure the imagery is relevant for an audience in 1905!

TOP TIP: This could be an ideal opportunity to design something using a computer and make a fantastic class display.

Where did you spend your holidays this year? Did you stay at home? Go to a relative's house? Go to the seaside? Or were you lucky enough to go to a warm sunny place on the other side of the world?

Time on our hands

The idea of families being able to 'go on holiday' is quite a new one. In 1800, few people had holidays. Sunday was most people's only day off, so the majority rested after they had been to church. Workers were given a day off for religious festivals (Christmas Day, Easter Sunday and so on) but these 'holy days' only amounted to a couple of days each year.

By 1850, things had started to change. People worked shorter hours than ever before, found themselves at home earlier in the evenings and off work on Saturday afternoons. All of a sudden, ordinary workers had enough leisure time to enjoy new sports and other pastimes, or even go away for short holidays to the seaside.

In 1871, Parliament introduced bank holidays, giving workers a few more days off throughout the year when banks and offices closed. Many people found themselves asking a question that they had never asked before: 'What am I going to do with my leisure time?'

FACT!

In order to make people thirsty for more beer, pub landlords would often put salt in their drinks. Interestingly, pubs today still try to encourage us to drink more by selling 'salty snacks' such as peanuts and crisps.

Let's go to the theatre

Without television, cinemas or games consoles, people had to go out to the theatre or a **music hall** to get their entertainment. There were posh theatres for listening to Shakespeare or opera, and cheaper ones for listening to **melodramas**. Melodramas were plays with really dramatic plots and lots of songs. A bit like a pantomime today, the audience were encouraged to boo and hiss at the villain and cheer for the hero.

Even cheaper than the cheap theatres were the music halls. A music hall was a large building where the audience would pay to see a wide variety of acts including singers, comedians, acrobats and magicians. The audience sang along with songs they recognized and shouted rude comments at performers they didn't like. Some music hall performers became the superstar celebrities of their day. Singer Marie Lloyd, for example, was mobbed when she appeared in public. She is most famous for singing 'My Old Man (Said Follow the Van)' and 'A Little of What You Fancy Does You Good'.

Shall we go to the pub?

When ordinary people had any time off work, many of them went to their local pub and drank heavily. In London, one house in every 77 was a pub and in parts of Newcastle there was one pub for every 22 families.

Hungry for More?

How do people spend their leisure time today? Think about the sorts of activities *you* do in your leisure time and compare them with the 1800s. Why not find out the sorts of things the average person does in their spare time in today's world? How have the activities changed? What's similar?

SOURCE A: *An audience and actors at a 'penny gaff' around 1870, a music hall to which the admission was a penny.*

SOURCE B: *A pub – or 'gin palace' as they were sometimes called – in the 1800s. It was a place to drink, fight, sing, gossip and gamble. Note the small child drinking too, something that was perfectly legal at the time.*

Work

1 a What is 'leisure time'?
   b Why did the amount of leisure time enjoyed by many people start to increase after 1850?

2 Explain the following terms:
   i   melodrama
   ii   music hall
   iii gin palace.

New crazes

Photography, reading comic books, cross-stitching (a type of embroidery), cycling, roller skating, having a 'shampoo' and head massage in a bath house, and listening to musicians in a bandstand at the local park were all popular in the 1800s. Reading books became more common too, as more people learned to read. Novels by authors such as Charles Dickens (who wrote *Oliver Twist*), Jane Austen (*Pride and Prejudice*), Robert Louis Stevenson (*Treasure Island*), Lewis Carroll (*Alice's Adventures in Wonderland*) and Mary Shelley (*Frankenstein*) sold thousands of copies.

New sports

For hundreds of years, people had been playing many of the sports we play today, but without any proper rules. And there were different versions of the same game in different parts of Britain. But with people having more leisure time, and with trains able to take players and spectators around the country, the sports had to become more organized. Players formed organizations to create standard rules and set up leagues and competitions. And soon watching sports was as popular as playing them.

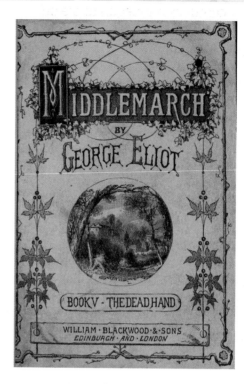

SOURCE A: *A copy of one of the most famous novels of all time, George Eliot's* Middlemarch *(1871–2). Writer George Eliot was, in fact, a woman by the name of Marian Evans. She used a man's name because she felt that if people thought she was a man, they would take her books seriously!*

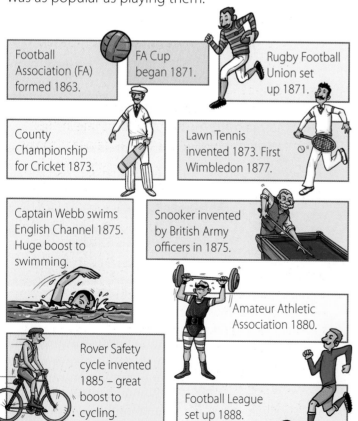

Football Association (FA) formed 1863.

FA Cup began 1871.

Rugby Football Union set up 1871.

County Championship for Cricket 1873.

Lawn Tennis invented 1873. First Wimbledon 1877.

Captain Webb swims English Channel 1875. Huge boost to swimming.

Snooker invented by British Army officers in 1875.

Amateur Athletic Association 1880.

Rover Safety cycle invented 1885 – great boost to cycling.

Football League set up 1888.

Blood sports

Betting on fighting animals – called **blood sports** – had been popular for centuries but began to die out in the 1800s. The RSPCA was set up in 1824 and bear baiting and cockfighting had both been banned by 1849.

A day at the seaside

The growth of the railways meant that ordinary people were able to travel away from the towns or the countryside. People would save up all year so they could go to coastal towns like Blackpool, Brighton, Southend or Margate. Hotels, amusement arcades, piers and promenades were built to entertain the thousands of 'day trippers' who travelled to these seaside towns in search of fun. And one of the first to realize that there was money to be made by organizing rail trips to Britain's beaches was a man called Thomas Cook, in 1841. It wasn't long before he was organizing week-long holidays too. The company he created still sells holidays today.

SOURCE B: *Ramsgate beach in July 1887. Can you see:*

i) *the pier?*
ii) *the Punch and Judy show?*
iii) *the ice-cream seller?*
iv) *the seafront hotels?*
v) *the 'bathing booths' (a sort of portable changing room that swimmers wheeled out into the sea)?*
vi) *the railway station, which brought visitors right up to the sea front?*

FACT!

The upper classes had always enjoyed plenty of leisure time. It was usual for the children of rich families, for example, to spend six months or more doing a 'Grand Tour' of Europe after they left school.

Work

1 Match up each date with the correct event.

1841	Rugby Football Union set up
1849	Football League set up
1871	Rover Safety cycle invented
1885	Thomas Cook starts his company
1888	Key blood sports banned by this date

2 How do *you* enjoy your leisure time in today's world? Make a list of what you do in your spare time. Then compare it to how people spent their spare time in the 1800s. What sports or pastimes are similar? What do you do that's different?

3 **a** What were 'blood sports'?
   b Why do you think these 'sports' gradually began to disappear?

4 Look at **Source B**.
   a Write a short description of this scene.
   b In what ways was the beach at Ramsgate in 1887 different from a typical British seaside beach today?

5 It is 1890. Plan a weekend's entertainment for you and your friend and write them a letter explaining how you will both spend your time:

TOP TIP: You want to make your friend excited about their visit, so your letter should be enthusiastically written!

- Will you watch any sports? If so, which ones?
- What about a day at the seaside? How will you get there? Which resort? What will you do?
- After visiting church, how will you spend Sunday afternoon? A walk in the park perhaps? What can you expect to do (and see) there?

The birth of modern football

Football is not a modern game: it has been popular in this country – and the rest of the world – for centuries. In the Middle Ages, for example, whole villages played against each other, trying to get a ball (which was usually a pig's bladder stuffed with straw) from the centre of one village to the other. There weren't any proper rules, teams just agreed them before they started, so sometimes players were allowed to handle the ball and at other times they weren't! Sometimes teams were restricted to 20 players per side, but mostly there was no limit to the number of people taking part (see **Source A**).

Mission Objective

- Analyse sources to establish how football developed in the nineteenth century.

Football remained a rough, tough, unorganized sport for many, many years. Then, in the 1800s, things began to change, and by 1900 football had become a highly organized, professional sport with carefully written laws, proper teams, leagues and competitions. Your task over the next few pages is to investigate these changes. Look through the sources very carefully to discover how football became the sport we recognize today.

SOURCE A: *A football match in the 1500s.*

'When football teams play each other it's important that both sides play by the same rules. At one time it was necessary to agree the rules before almost every match. The Football Association was formed in 1863 by several London clubs to develop a permanent set of rules… the rules agreed by the FA said, among other things, that you couldn't use your hands unless you were a goalie.'

SOURCE B: *From* Victorians *by Bob Fowke, 2003.*

'By 1867 an FA handbook advised that matches should try "to have one side with striped jerseys [shirts] of one colour, say red, and the other with another, say blue". By the 1870s, strips were becoming part of the game with many clubs, such as Blackburn Rovers, adopting designs that remain unchanged to this day.'

▲ **SOURCE C:** *Adapted from an article entitled 'Football's equipment evolution' on the FIFA website (www.fifa.com).*

Date	Event
1863	Length of pitch, size of goals, kicks offs and bans on tripping up other players and picking up the ball are amongst the first 'laws'
1866	Ball size fixed
1870	Only 11 players allowed per team
1872	Referee first used (but only to keep time)
1872	First international between England and Scotland
1873	Free kick awarded for handball
1874	First use of shin pads
1874	Referees given power to send off players
1875	Crossbar used instead of tape
1878	Referees used whistle for the first time
1882	Two-handed throw-in introduced
1885	Highest ever score recorded in a British game. Arbroath beat Bon Accord in the Scottish Cup 36-0.
1889	Ball weight fixed
1891	Goal nets used for the first time
1891	Penalty kick introduced

▲ **SOURCE D:** *The laws of Association Football (as it is correctly known – the word 'soccer' comes from the word 'as**soc**iation') continue to change to this day. Here are some key changes in its early development.*

'In 1871 the FA announced the introduction of the FA Cup. It was the first knockout competition of its type in the world. Only 12 teams took part in the competition and it was won by The Wanderers.'

▲ **SOURCE E:** *The birth of the FA Cup, adapted from an article called 'History of Football', www.spartacus. schoolnet.co.uk.*

'The first football league was set up by 12 "founding" clubs in 1888. It was a massive success and, with workers having Saturday afternoon off, the matches drew huge crowds. The railways enabled "fans" to travel to matches and they could keep up with their team's fortunes through the national newspapers. The fact that very little equipment was needed and that it could be played in any weather meant that even the poorest could afford to play and it soon became known as the "people's game". Its popularity was confirmed in 1901, when a massive crowd of over 110,000 watched the FA Cup Final.'

▲ **SOURCE F:** *A modern historian, 2008. Teams were formed in all sorts of ways. For example, Wolves and Stoke City were formed by ex-schoolchildren looking to fill their time, whilst Sunderland was formed by teachers.*

Work

1 **The Big Write!**

You work at the National Football Museum in Manchester and have been told that a group of primary school children are coming to visit. You've been asked to speak to them for three minutes about the development of football. You also have to give them a leaflet to take away. Plan your speech and design the leaflet. Why not work with a partner or in a small group?

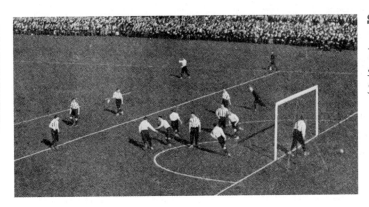

SOURCE G: *The 1901 FA Cup Final; Tottenham Hotspur score against Sheffield United.*

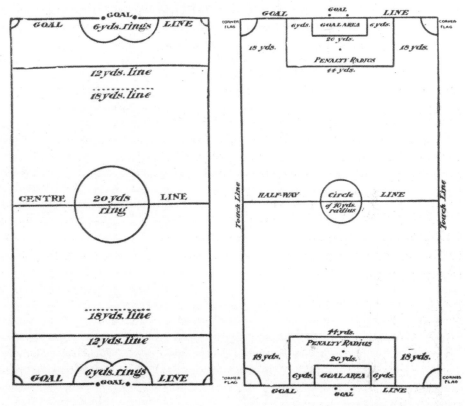

The field in 1892   The perfected playing pitch in 1905.

▲ **SOURCE H:** *The development of the football pitch. The picture on the left shows how the pitches were marked out up to 1905. You might be more familiar with how the pitch is marked out in the right-hand diagram.*

	P	W	D	L	F	A	Pts
Preston North End	22	18	4	0	74	15	40
Aston Villa	22	12	5	5	61	43	29
Wolverhampton Wanderers	22	12	4	6	50	37	28
Blackburn Rovers	22	10	6	6	66	45	26
Bolton Wanderers	22	10	2	10	63	59	22
West Bromwich Albion	22	10	2	10	40	46	22
Accrington	22	6	8	8	48	48	20
Everton	22	9	2	11	35	46	20
Burnley	22	7	3	12	42	62	17
Derby County	22	7	2	13	41	60	16
Notts County	22	5	2	15	39	73	12
Stoke	22	4	4	14	26	51	12

▲ **SOURCE I:** *The final standings for the first ever football league. It was such a success that a second and third division were soon formed.*

By 1901, about 80 per cent of the population lived in towns or cities… and they all needed a place to shop! It wasn't long before 'high-street shopping' became common. This painting, by Louise Rayner, is of Eastgate Street in Chester in the late 1800s. It is a great example of what a Victorian city high street would have looked like. The labels below this painting will help you to understand what's going on.

Mission Objectives

- Understand what a typical Victorian high street might have looked like.
- Investigate where some of our most famous high-street shops began.

SOURCE A: *Look out for the following:*

i) Pavements
From the 1850s, many high-street pavements were improved. By 1860 the first street cleaners had been employed.

ii) The tramlines
Horse-drawn tramcars ran on fixed rails along the cobblestone streets. By 1890, electric trams replaced the horse-drawn ones.

iii) Street traders
As well as the shops, people could buy from street traders or **costermongers**, as they were known. Can you see the costermongers in the painting?

iv) Shops
All sorts of goods could be bought in town and city centres. What sort of shops and goods can you see for sale in this painting?

v) Street lights
In high streets by 1835.

vi) Rich men, poor men
The high street was a mixture of all types of people. Can you see the upper-class men having a chat? What about the poor boys (one looking bored; the other staring through a shop window)?

New high-street shops

Up until the 1800s, goods were mainly sold in separate shops; for example, each selling just shoes, hats, coats, ribbons, underwear or shirts. So you'd go to one shop for your shoes (the shoe shop), another for a hat (the hat shop), another for a coat (the coat shop) and so on. But by the middle of the century, a few shops began to grow into what we call department stores, selling lots of different types of goods under one roof. Some, like Debenhams and John Lewis, still exist today.

The 1800s saw the birth of many of our familiar high-street shops. William Henry Smith (1848), John Sainsbury (1869), Jesse Boot (1871), Michael Marks and Tom Spencer (1894) all started trading at this time.

SOURCE B: *An early Sainsbury's store. By 1880, the invention of refrigeration meant that meat could be shipped from Australia and New Zealand without going mouldy. 'Fridges' inside shops meant that meat, milk and fish could be stored easily.*

New ideas on the high street

In 1844, 28 workers from Rochdale, Lancashire, each saved up to buy a stock of food and open a shop of their own. Workers sold their goods at fair prices and shared the profits out amongst their customers. Their co-operation with each other gave its name to their first shop – 'The Co-operative'. Today, 'Co-ops' exist all around the country.

FACT!

In 1875, the Sale of Food and Drugs Act allowed local councils to check the quality of food. The first inspectors found amazing tricks of the trade being used to fool customers (like mixing river water with milk or putting sawdust into flour!). Gradually, food quality improved.

Wise Up Words

costermonger

What Happened When? 1869

In the same year Sainsbury's began, 1869, the 'whirlwind' vacuum cleaner was invented by Ives W McGaffey.

Work

1 List some of the well-known shops that appeared in Victorian high streets between 1848 and 1894.

2 a How did 'The Co-operative' chain of stores get its name?
   b How did the 1875 Sale of Food and Drugs Act make things safer for customers?
   c How did the invention of refrigeration help:
   i shop owners?
   ii customers?

3 Prepare an information panel for the gallery in which Louise Rayner's painting hangs. The panel, which will be stuck to the wall next to the painting, will:
   • start with a basic description
   • explain what the painting tells the viewer about life in Victorian Britain – use details from the scene to help you
   • explain why it is important to look after and preserve paintings like this.

SOURCE C: *An early 'Co-op' shop in Woolwich, 1906.*

9.8 Why is there a chimpanzee on a £2 coin?

In 2009, the Bank of England (the organization that makes coins and banknotes) released a new £2 coin. The Queen was on one side and on the reverse was a picture of a man named Charles Darwin… and he was facing a chimpanzee! The same man, Charles Darwin, has also appeared on a £10 note! So who on earth is he? Why was he chosen to appear on banknotes and coins? And why are his achievements still remembered today?

Mission Objectives

- Explain Darwin's theory of evolution.
- Propose why Darwin's theory caused so much controversy.

Charles Darwin was born in 1809, the son of a doctor from Shrewsbury. At this time, the majority of people believed that the Bible was from God, and therefore contained literal truths. Most people were convinced that God had created the world complete with birds, fish, reptiles and other creatures – and then created humans – in seven days. And all these creatures, and humans, had been like that for all time, and that's how they would stay! In fact, as Darwin was growing up, very few people would ever dream of disagreeing with this creation story. But in 1859, Charles Darwin published a book that gave a different explanation… and shocked the world! Read his story carefully.

SOURCE A: *The Darwin £2 coin, and the £10 note that features his face.*

1 In 1831, Darwin got a job as a scientist on board a ship. The ship had to travel the world finding out as much about far-off lands as possible.

Darwin collected all sorts of plants, animals, insects and rocks. The voyage took him all around the world.

2 In 1835, the ship arrived at a small group of islands called the Galapagos Islands in the Pacific Ocean.

The islands were 965km off the coast of South America.

3 Whilst there, Darwin noticed that some birds, cut off from each other on different islands, were identical… apart from their beaks!

ISLAND A

ISLAND B

This got Darwin thinking!

4 Darwin investigated the islands some more and looked at the food the different looking birds were eating.

> Darwin thought that the type of beak the bird had depended on the food that was available on their island.

So the bird that has only seeds available develops a big, strong beak for cracking seeds… and the bird on another island develops a long curved beak for reaching down into cactus flowers.

5 Darwin arrived home after nearly five years at sea. He spent the next few years thinking long and hard about the bird beaks, and then wrote a book!

In 1859, Darwin's *On the Origin of Species* was published. In it, he proposed a new theory about how life develops. He suggested that all living things had evolved (kept changing ever so slightly) over millions and millions of years, and only those best suited to their environments survived and reproduced!

6 To use giraffes as an example, Darwin said that Giraffe B, which can reach tall trees, will be more likely to survive than Giraffe A, which will starve and die.

Giraffe B would survive (because it can feed itself) and reproduce. It would probably mate with another tall giraffe (who had survived), so their baby giraffe would have a long neck too… and over millions of years, giraffes would all have long necks!

7 Darwin's theory shocked the world!

According to Darwin, animals had not been created at the beginning of time in the way that people had always thought – animals were changing (or evolving) all the time!

8 Darwin's next book caused even more controversy.

In 1871, Darwin published *The Descent of Man*. In it, he claimed that man evolved gradually from apes over millions of years!

9 *The Descent of Man* suggested that humans weren't created by God – they were actually just advanced apes!

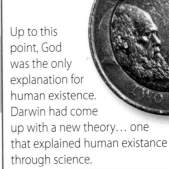

Up to this point, God was the only explanation for human existence. Darwin had come up with a new theory… one that explained human existance through science.

10 Darwin's theories are still controversial, and many people completely disagree with him. But his ideas are definitely thought-provoking – and taught in science classes all over the world today!

When he died in 1882 he was buried in Westminster Abbey alongside great minds such as Isaac Newton and Charles Dickens. And on the 200th anniversary of his birth his image was put onto a £2 coin… next to an ape!

Work

1. ✏ Produce your own diagram or poster that explains Darwin's theory of evolution. Use pictures where appropriate and try not to use any more than 100 words. Aim it at someone younger than you!
2. Why do you think Darwin's theories were so controversial?
3. a Why do you think Darwin was chosen to go on a £10 note and a £2 coin?
   b If you were asked to choose a person to go on a new note, who would it be? Make sure you give sensible reasons for your choice (and it can't be yourself!).

The Great Hunger

In 1997, the British Prime Minister at the time, Tony Blair, made a statement on behalf of the government, in County Cork. He said that the government was sorry for something that happened in Ireland over 150 years before. Mr Blair said that one million Irish people died as a result of something the English did! (See **Source A**.) But what was he talking about? Was his statement accurate? And do you think politicians in today's world should apologize for the actions of those long ago?

Mission Objectives

- Investigate the causes of the Great Hunger.
- Judge whether the British government did enough to help.

'One million people died in what was then part of the richest and most powerful nation in the world. This still causes pain today. Those who governed in London at the time failed their people through standing by while a crop failure turned into a massive human tragedy...'

SOURCE A: *Part of Tony Blair's statement, 1997.*

The British in Ireland

In 1840, over eight million people lived in Ireland. Over half were poor peasants who rented tiny farms from landowners. Many of these landowners were English, from families that had taken the land from the Irish many years before. Now the Irish had to rent land that had once belonged to them! This made them angry. Most of these peasants lived on nothing but the potatoes they grew in their fields. They couldn't even afford bread.

Since 1801, Britain had ruled Ireland from London. The British Parliament made all the decisions relating to Ireland, yet British laws meant that Catholics couldn't vote. As most of the poor Irish peasants were Catholics, this also made them angry.

Famine

In September 1845, a potato disease called **blight** started to destroy the potato crop. Millions were left without their main source of food. The same thing happened in 1846, 1847 and 1848. By the end of 1848, nearly a million people had died of starvation. Another million left Ireland altogether for a new life in America. By 1871, one quarter of New York's population was Irish!

Over to you!

As you can imagine, the Great Hunger (as this famine was known) is a very significant event in Irish history. And people all over the world (not just in Ireland) have all sorts of opinions about it. Some say that the British government acted terribly at this time and didn't do anything to help the Irish. Others say that the British government did a bit to help… but not enough. Some have even argued that the British actually tried to *kill* the Irish and have likened it to the way the Nazis tried to kill Jews during World War Two. But what do you think? Read through the wide variety of sources over the next few pages and work through the questions in the Work section on p.165. You will then be asked to form your own opinion.

'Families, when all was eaten and had no hope left, took their last look at the sun, built up their cottage doors so that none might see them die nor hear the groans, and were found weeks afterwards, skeletons on their own hearths.'

SOURCE B: *From an eyewitness account at the time of the* **famine**, *quoted in* The World of Empire, Industry and Trade, 2000.

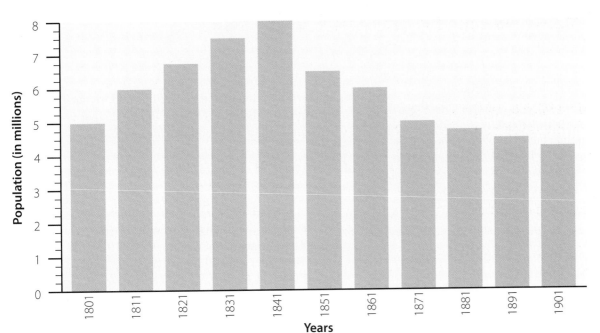

SOURCE C: *Estimated population of Ireland, 1801–1901.*

'The British Government was slow to give help. Worse still, it gave no protection to peasant farmers who were too poor to pay rents on their land. Many were **evicted** [thrown out] from their homes by the landowners, most of whom lived in England.'

▲ **SOURCE D:** *Written by the modern historian, Andrew Langley, in* Victorian England, *1994.*

What Happened When? `1845`

In the same year as the potato blight, Thomas Barnardo, the famous Irish philanthropist, was born in Dublin. He became the founder of Barnardo's, Britain's largest children's charity today (see page 139).

SOURCE E: *An Irish family waiting to be evicted from their home for not paying their rent.*

'One of the greatest natural disasters to strike the Western World in modern times, the potato famine that hit Ireland... resulted in more than one million deaths and the forced migration of a million more. Its effects would not have been a tenth as bad if the British Government of the time had made the slightest effort to relieve the starvation, and if... landlords had not made matters worse by evicting thousands of tenants from the land.'

▲ **SOURCE A:** *Written by the modern historian, Duncan Gunn, in* The Little Book of British History, *1999.*

'He [the British prime minister, Robert Peel] had ordered Indian corn and meal to be bought and handed out to the starving Irish. He initiated [started] public work schemes so that poor labourers could earn money... assistance in Ireland was limited to public works programmes [but] the schemes couldn't cope with the numbers, so were abandoned in favour of indoor relief, soup kitchens and workhouses... many were helped by voluntary workers. The Quakers [a Christian group] set up soup kitchens, the Guinness brewing family provided food and work, the British Relief Association gave funds and the New York Irish Relief Fund sent nearly £250,000.'

▲ **SOURCE B:** *Written by the modern historian, Bea Stimpson, in* The World of Empire, Industry and Trade, *2000.*

'It is my opinion that too much has been done for the Irish people. Under such treatment the people have grown worse instead of better... it is not the job of Government to give people food.'

▲ **SOURCE C:** *Written by a British government official in 1847. The man was actually in charge of the Famine Relief Association.*

Year	Exports (wheat sent out of Ireland)	Imports (wheat sent into Ireland)
1844	424	30
1845	513	28
1846	284	197
1847	146	889
1848	314	439

'I know where the blame lies for this and we must face the truth. We should not forgive the English or forget this happened. They were to blame for the famine.'

▲ **SOURCE D:** *Adapted from a speech given by Mr Andrews, speaking in the Irish Parliament in 1995.*

'I do not think the English Government tried to kill the Irish. There were famines in England at this time and the Government ignored them too, and left the people to die. This is what they were like in those days. They thought it was not the Government's job to feed people.'

▲ **SOURCE E:** *Adapted from a speech made by Mr Connor, talking in the Irish Parliament in 1995.*

Ireland and Home Rule

After the famine, many Irish people felt that the British government hadn't done enough to help. Some wanted to be free of British rule and wanted Ireland to be independent. This was known as **Home Rule**. One Irish group, known as **Fenians**, were even prepared to use violence to get what they wanted. One British prime minister, William Gladstone, actually supported the Irish in their quest for independence and twice tried to get Parliament to agree to Irish Home Rule. However, both times the politicians in London voted against it... and Ireland remained part of the UK!

Be a Top Historian

Top historians understand that there are many, many topics in history that are controversial. The Great Hunger is one of those topics – and you can see from **Sources J** and **K** that the topic still arouses fierce debate in the modern world. So it is well worth studying in History lessons.

SOURCE F: *Wheat imports and exports to Ireland, 1844–1848 (in thousand tons).*

SOURCE G: *This statue remembering the famine was erected in 1998 in Boston, USA. It was paid for by the Irish descendants of those who emigrated in the 1840s. In some parts of the USA, schoolteachers were instructed to teach students that the actions of the British government in Ireland in the 1840s were similar to the actions of the Nazis against the Jews during the 1930s and 1940s.*

Work

1 a How did many Irish people feel about the British, even before the famine? Explain your answer carefully.
   b Why was the potato so important to many Irish people?
2 a What do **Sources B**, **C**, **D**, and **E** on pages 162–163 tell you about how Irish people suffered during the famine?
   b How did some people escape from the famine?
3 Look at **Source A** on page 164.
   a According to this source, did the British government make any effort at all to help the Irish people?
   b Do you think this is true? What evidence is there in **Sources B** and **F** on page 164 that might help you answer this?
4 According to **Source E**, why did the British government do so little to help people?

5 Look at **Source G**.
   a Why do you think so many Americans are interested in the famine?
   b Do you think the British government's actions during the famine were as bad as the Nazis' attempts to kill all Jewish people?
6 Hold a class debate. Your debate should focus on two areas:
   i   Did the British *try* to kill the Irish people?
   ii Was Tony Blair right to apologize for the famine?
   Your teacher will help you to organize and structure your preparation and discussions.
7 a What is Home Rule?
   b Can you suggest reasons why the idea of Home Rule was so popular amongst some of the Irish population at this time?

How did Britain change between 1745 and 1901?

This book covers the years 1745 to 1901. During this time, some amazing and lasting changes took place. It was a period in British history when great industrial towns and cities appeared, full of people linked together by roads, canals and trains that ran through the countryside. By 1901, most people were better fed and clothed, healthier and more educated than anyone could have imagined in 1745. Shops contained goods from all over the world, brought to Britain on huge steamships, which stood in newly built docks. But there were still many issues and problems too, many of which would not be dealt with for many years. Read this section carefully. It doesn't feature all the changes, discoveries and innovations that took place between 1745 and 1901 but it tries to pick out some of the most important and interesting ones.

Mission Objective

Examine the extent that Britain changed between 1745 and 1901 in key areas such as population, transport, politics, leisure, health and medicine.

Travel

1745: Very slow. London to Edinburgh took two weeks by road... and the roads were terrible!

1901: Much faster. London to Edinburgh, took nine hours by train. The roads were better... and the motor car had been invented (but they were only for the very rich because they were so expensive).

Population

1745: Seven million
80 per cent lived in the countryside.

1901: 37 million
80 per cent lived in towns and cities.

Leisure time

1745: Working people had very few holidays. Blood sports very popular.

1901: Working people enjoyed shorter working hours and, therefore, more leisure time. Sports became more organized.

Politics

1745: Only 5 per cent of the population could vote in elections. No women could vote.

1901: Now most men could vote but still no women.

Law and order

1901: A professional police force and the death penalty only for very serious crimes. Prisons reformed and transportation stopped.

1745: No police force and the death penalty for lots of crimes. Transportation also common.

Health and medicine

1745: People did not know that germs caused disease. If a person reached the age of one, they might expect to live to the age of 40. Operations were very dangerous.

1901: Knowledge that germs caused disease. Inventions such as vaccinations, anticeptic and anaesthetics meant that if you reached the age of one you might expect to live to the age of 55.

Work

1745: The farming industry was the largest employer, particularly for wool and food production. Manufacturing took place on a small scale, often in people's homes. Wind, horse, water and hand power was used.

1901: Industry was dominated by coal, iron, steel and cloth. Steam-powered factories were a common sight.

The British Empire

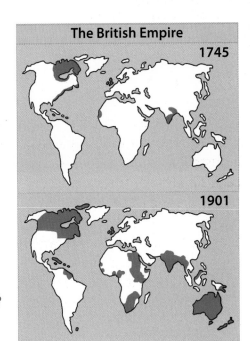

1745

1901

Education

1745: In England, most children did not go to school and few could read or write. In Scotland there were lots of schools and many people were literate. School was not compulsory.

1901: School was compulsory for all 5–12 year olds. Newspaper and book publishing was expanding.

Food

1745: Bread, cheese, meat and vegetables were the main foods. All meals were made at home.

1901: Frozen meat and fish, foreign fruit, tinned and packet food were introduced.

🖊 The Big Write!

Hungry for More?

One of the world's most famous newspapers, *The Times*, first appeared on sale in 1785. In small groups, produce your own version of *The Times* but write it to cover the whole period of 1745–1901. Write articles for each of the following headlines:

- Living and working
- Health news
- The fight for rights
- Women's page
- Crime and punishment
- The Empire
- Sports pages
- Getting around
- Designers, inventors and engineers.

You are writing in the year 1901, so you will need to remind yourself who your audience is.

Work

1 a Copy one of the sentences below that best describes Britain in 1901:

- Britain had changed completely between 1745 and 1901.
- Britain had changed a lot by 1901 but some things had not changed.
- Britain had not changed at all between 1745 and 1901.

b Explain why you have made your choice.

2 Divide a page, or a sheet of paper, into three: one-third for 1745, one-third for 1901 and one-third for today. Using the headings from the ten boxes on these pages, compare life in Britain during 1745, 1901 and today. You can use drawings and/or writing, and you may have to do some extra research for some of the figures (for example, population figures of today).

2 Why not find out more about some of the products mentioned on this page? Prepare fact files on some (or all) of them.

Assessing Your Learning 3

Why should we remember them?

Good historians are able to identify what makes a person **significant**. This is your chance to have a go at doing this.

Imagine that money has been raised to design and build a new statue to commemorate a significant person from the period of time covered in this book (1745–1901). It's your job to decide who should be considered! There are lots of different theories about what makes a person 'significant' – but the vital ingredients listed below should help you decide when choosing your person.

Use the following questions – or criteria – when thinking about your chosen person:

- How important was this person's work at the time?

- Did their work last for a long time?

- Are we still affected by their work?

- Did their work improve society at all?

The person you choose as your statue might be a king or a queen, or an inventor, scientist, writer or politician… but they must be **significant**!

TO BE UNVEILED SOON !

Task 1

Your first challenge is to identify your significant person! There are some examples given below – but you may wish to choose your own.

Sir Richard Arkwright	Edward Jenner
Jane Austen	Samuel Johnson
Charles Babbage	John Snow
Joseph Bazalgette	George Stephenson
Annie Besant	James Watt
I K Brunel	Josiah Wedgewood
Josephine Butler	Duke of Wellington
Thomas Clarkson	Napoleon Bonaparte
James Cook	William Wilberforce
William Cuffay	Horatio Nelson
Charles Darwin	Florence Nightingale
Charles Dickens	Fergus O'Connor
Benjamin Disraeli	Robert Peel
George Eliot	Charles Parnell
Olaudah Equiano	Louis Pasteur
Michael Faraday	Mary Seacole
William Gladstone	Adam Smith
John Howard	Granville Sharp
Thomas Huxley	

Task 2

Now it's time to carry out some research. You might do this by looking through this Student Book, or by visiting a library or searching online.

Be a Top Historian

Be careful when searching online. Don't just go to one website and get all your information from it. Use a variety of websites and use evidence from books to build up a picture of your significant person. Try websites like www.bbc.co.uk to start with.

Sir Richard Arkwright.

Annie Besant.

Isambard Kingdom Brunel.

Horatio Nelson.

Olaudah Equiano.

Task 3

When you have all your information, your next step is to complete an extended piece of writing. The aim with this piece of writing is to convince someone that your chosen person is worthy of a statue! It must:

- Have a title, for example 'Why (your chosen person's name) should have a statue'.

- Include basic, factual information about their life, for example; when and where they were born, key jobs, roles, beliefs, etc.

- Outline different events in their life.

- Give your opinion as to why your chosen person should be remembered today. Use the criteria on page 168 to justify why they are a significant person who should be commemorated with a statue.

TOP TIP: Write persuasively about your favourite, trying to convince others that he or she deserves the award. Use powerful adjectives that will make them seem great, for example, '_____ was amazing because…'. Mention how important their contribution was to the period. For example, '_____ was important because…'.

Hungry for More?

Be creative! How would your chosen person's statue look? What is their pose? What objects are they holding? Explain why you have chosen to depict your person in this way.

Assessing your work

Look at the success criteria for this task to help you plan and evaluate your work.

Good	In a **good** response, you would…	• provide a basic outline of the person's life • use dates and historical terms correctly • explain why the person was important or significant • have started to produce structured work.
Better	In a **better** response, you would…	• provide an outline of the person's life, including dates and historical terms • select and use information to explain why the person was significant, using correct historical terms • produce properly structured work.
Best	In the **best** response, you would…	• provide an accurate outline of the person's life • explain in detail why the person should be remembered and how their actions and achievements changed lots of people's lives, mentioning short- or long-term changes, or both • show how you made your decisions about what was significant about the person's life • select, organize and use relevant information, using the correct historical terms to produce structured work • show where you got your information from.

Glossary

Abdicate To give up power

Abolish Bring to an end; for example, the slave trade

Alcoholic Someone who is addicted to alcohol

American War of Independence A war in 1775; British people who lived in settlements in America decided they wanted to be 'Americans' and fought against troops from Great Britain for their independence; the British surrendered in 1781 and the Americans were granted their independence

Amputate To cut off a part of the body, such as a leg or arm

Anaesthetic A substance that stops you feeling pain

Antiseptic A chemical that prevents infection by killing germs

Aqueduct A bridge that carries a canal over an obstacle (such as a river)

Artillery Soldiers who fight with firearms

Auction A public sale in which goods are sold to the person who offers the highest price

Back-to-back housing Rows of houses built very close together without room for a garden

Bearer A mining job; children who carried coal-sacks around the pit

Blight A type of disease which infects and destroys crops, for example, potatoes

Blood sport Watching and betting on fighting animals; the craze began to die out in the 1850s

Board of Health A group set up in some towns to investigate how the disease cholera spread and how it could be prevented

Bow Street Runners The forerunners of the police force; a group of men who were paid to capture as many criminals as possible

Branded Permanently marked, using a hot metal instrument to burn the skin; used to show who owned slaves

British Empire The collection of countries and colonies (areas) that Britain ruled over; at its height, Britain ruled over 450 million people of different nationalities, living in 56 colonies around the world

Broadsides All the guns along one side of a warship; often all fired at the same time

Canal A long, narrow, man-made channel of water

Capital crime A crime that is punished by the death penalty

Cartridge A type of casing that contains a bullet or an explosive

Cast iron Iron that has been heated into a liquid and placed in a mould to make a shape

Census An official count of the population, done every ten years in Britain

Chartist A member of a campaign group of ordinary working men who wanted to bring about changes to the voting system; they issued the 'People's Charter' in 1838

Chloroform A strong smelling liquid that was used as an anaesthetic

Cholera A disease caused by infected food or water; victims suffer from diarrhoea, vomiting and can die

Climbing boy A child, often an orphan, who worked for an adult chimney sweep; they would be small enough to climb up chimneys and clean them

Clothier A person who buys and sells wool/cloth

Coalface The area where coal is dug out of the ground

Coke Coal that has been heated to remove the sulphur; used to make cast iron

Commuting Travelling to work

Constable A unpaid person, who tried to keep law and order in his town for the period of one year

Constipation A health condition in which the sufferer has difficulty going to the toilet, usually because of hardened faeces

Contaminate To make something impure by infecting it with an unclean or dangerous substance

Costermonger A street trader

Dame school A basic school run by women, often in the front room of their house; students paid a few pennies to attend

Declaration of the Rights of Man A list made during the French Revolution which stated 'rights' that every man should have

Dehydrate To lose a large amount of water from the body

Domestic system The system where people worked in their homes or small workshops rather than in factories

Drawer A mining job; children who pushed and pulled loaded coal wagons in the pit

Ducking Stool A form of punishment for nagging wives, organised by their husbands, whereby a woman would be tied to a stool and 'ducked' into water

Dysentery A deadly form of diarrhoea

Entrepreneur A business person who takes risks, often with their own money, in order to make a profit

Epidemic Rapid spread of a disease

Ether A colourless liquid that was used as an anaesthetic

Evict To expel or throw out someone from a property

Exile To expel someone from their home country

Factory system The system where people worked in factories to produce goods in large numbers; replaced the domestic system

Famine An extreme shortage of food

Fenian A member of an Irish group, the Fenians, who vigorously campaigned for Ireland's independence from Britain

Flying Shuttle A 1733 invention in the cloth industry; this machine sped up weaving

French Revolution A period of rebellion in France, starting in 1789, whereby poor French people rebelled against the king and his rich followers

Gallows A wooden frame used for hanging criminals

Greenwich Mean Time The name given to British time when it was standardized in 1852; the local time in Greenwich (London) began to be used for the whole country

Guillotine A machine with a blade, used to cut off a person's head

Highwayman A type of robber who targeted people travelling on roads

Home Rule When decisions about the government of a country are made by the citizens themselves

Immigrant Someone who travels to a foreign country in order to settle there

Immigration People travelling to a foreign country in order to settle there

Independence Existing separately from other people or things; an independent nation is not controlled by another country

Indifferent Not bothered; showing no interest; poor quality

Industrial Revolution A complete change in the way things were made; a time when factories replaced farming as the main form of business in Britain; sometimes used to describe the changes in population, transport, cities and so on in the period between 1745 and 1901

Industry The work and methods involved in making things in factories

Infantry Foot soldiers

Inferior Worse, or less important

Invader A person (or group) who enters a place in order to take over

Ironworks A factory that makes things from iron

Lashed Whipped

Literacy Ability to read and write

Locomotive An engine used to pull trucks or passenger carriages along a track

Logbook An official record of a school

Lunar Society A group of men who discussed how to use new developments in science to improve people's lives

Magistrate An unpaid volunteer who worked in courts and questioned suspects about crimes

Manufacture Make goods in a factory

Marine A soldier, mainly serving at sea

Maternity Relating to or involving pregnant women and birth

Mechanized Work done by machine

Melodrama Musical plays with very dramatic plots and exaggerated emotions

Metropolitan Police A force of ex-soldiers and men, set up in 1829, to enforce law and order on the streets of London

Middle Passage The middle part of the slave trade triangle; a long journey, during which African men, women and children were taken by ship from Africa to the Americas

Midwife A nurse trained to help women at the birth of a baby

Miner A worker who digs coal out of the ground

Music hall A venue which puts on a wide variety of entertainment acts; cheaper to visit than a theatre

Mutiny Refusing to follow the orders of a person in authority

Muzzle A cover or strap that covers up the nose and mouth

Native American The tribespeople who have lived on the continent of North America for thousands of years

Navvy A worker employed to build roads, railways, canals or buildings

Nelson's touch A method of attack by Horatio Nelson, whereby British ships cut through enemy lines at an angle and fired, rather than drawing alongside them in the traditional way

Okra A tropical plant with long, green, edible pods

Overseer A man in charge of the factory workers on a day-to-day basis, like a manager

Pasteurization Heating of food and drink, for example, milk, to kill germs

Pauper apprentice A orphan who worked in a factory in return for food and a bed

Peterloo Massacre A violent event in 1819; British soldiers were sent by the government to St Peter's Field, Manchester, to break up a big meeting of people who were campaigning for votes for all; eleven members of the crowd were killed and 400 were injured

Philanthropist Someone who freely gives help or money to people in need

Phosphorus A poisonous chemical that ignites easily

Plantation A huge farm that grows cotton, sugar, tobacco, and so on; a plantation owner normally used slaves to do the work

Power loom A machine invented by Edmund Cartwright which was used to weave cloth at greater speed

Protest An event organised by people who would like to officially state their unhappiness about a particular issue, usually against the government; protests can be peaceful, but can also become violent

Ragged school A charity school which was free to attend for very poor children

Raking Firing along the length of something, for example, a line of ships

Raw material Natural substances such as coal, iron, ore, gold, oil and so on

Reform Make changes to an organization or government

Reformer A person who campaigns for change to an organization or government

Reign of Terror A time in the 1790s, after the French Revolution, when many of those who had opposed the French Revolution were executed

Revolt A violent attempt by a group of people to change the people who rule them

Revolution The overthrow of one rule or government and its replacement with another

Rotary motion Turning or spinning machinery

Scramble A method of buying slaves; a price is agreed before the buyers rush into a cage to grab the best slave they can

Sepoy An Indian soldier serving British authorities

Sepsis Poisoning or infection

Seven Years War A war between Britain and France for territory in America in the 1750s and 60s

Sexist Discrimination against a person because of gender

Sharpshooter A type of gunman who stayed on his own ship and shot at the enemy from a distance

Six Acts Laws introduced by the British government after the Peterloo Massacre in 1819, which tightened up on protests and campaign meetings

Slave trade triangle A three-legged trading journey; traders left Britain with goods, travelling to Africa to trade those goods for slaves, then they travelled to the Americas to trade the slaves for more goods, which they then took back to Britain

Sniper A highly trained gunman who shoots at enemies from a hidden location

Social pyramid A name given to the structure of society; the richest people are at the very top of the pyramid, with the working class at the very bottom

Spinning frame A machine invented by Richard Arkwright in 1769 which produced good, strong thread very quickly; powered by waterwheel; also called a 'water frame'

Spinning Jenny A 1764 invention in the cloth industry, this machine made the production of thread quicker by spinning more threads at the same time

Spinning mule A machine invented by Samuel Crompton in 1779 which produced high quality thread for the cloth industry

Squalor The state of being very dirty and run-down

Stagecoach A large, horse-drawn vehicle carrying people from one place to another

Steam engine An engine that uses steam as a means of power

Sterilize To clean an object so that it is free from any germs

Suburb An area of a town or city away from the centre

'Sun-and-planet' gear system A system used to turn the wheel in a steam engine

Terrace A row of houses

Toll An amount of money charged for using a stretch of road or a bridge

Toll keeper A person who collected money (tolls) so that travellers could use a turnpike road

Transportation A punishment; guilty criminals could be sent to a far away land for a period of five, seven or 14 years

Trapper A mining job; children who opened and closed trapdoors in the pit

Turnpike trust A group of businessmen who improved and maintained a stretch of road and charged people to use it

Tutor A teacher

Vaccination The process of giving someone a vaccine (a substance made from the germs that cause a disease), usually by injection, which protects them against disease by making them immune to it

Viaduct A long, high bridge that carries a road or railway over an obstacle, such as a valley or river

Viceroy Someone who rules in another country or colony on behalf of the monarch

Watchman A paid volunteer who tried to catch criminals

Water frame A machine invented by Richard Arkwright in 1769 which produced good, strong thread very quickly; powered by waterwheel; also called a 'spinning frame'

Workhouse A type of building in each town in the 1800s where poor people were kept and forced to work in harsh conditions

Wrought iron Iron that has been heated up and hammered into shape; more flexible than cast iron

Yam A vegetable that grows in hot regions; also called a sweet potato

Index

NOTES TO HELP YOU USE THIS INDEX:

Kings, queens and other royals are listed by their first name, so look for 'Victoria, Queen' and not 'Queen Victoria'. All other people are listed by their surname, so look for 'Brunel, Isambard Kingdom' and not 'Isambard Kingdom Brunel'.

A

abdicate/abdication 108
abolishing slavery 88–91
Albert, Prince 48, 59
alcoholics 13, 52, 74
American War of Independence 96–97
amputate/amputation 144, 145
anaesthetics 13, 144, 146
antiseptics 13, 146, 147
aqueducts 34
Arkwright, Richard 16, 17, 41
artillery 109
auction of slaves 84

B

Babbage, Charles 43
back-to-back housing 54
Barnardo, Thomas 139, 163
Battle of Trafalgar 102–105
Bazalgette, Joseph 64
bearers 27
Bell, Alexander Graham 45
Besant, Annie 132–133
Bessemer, Henry 44
'black gold' 26–27
blight 162
blood sports 155
Boards of Health 60, 61
Bonaparte, Napoleon 99–101, 108–111
Booth, William 138
Boulton, Matthew 20, 21, 42
Bow Street Runners 70
branded/branding 80, 85
Bridgewater, Duke of 34
Brindley, James 35
British Empire 92–97, 112–121
broadsides 103
Brunel, Isambard Kingdom 44

C

Cadbury company 149–151
canals 34–35
capital crimes 68
cartridges 118–119
cast iron 28
census/censuses 12
Chadwick, Edwin 61–62
changing Britain 164–165
Chartists 129–131
chloroform 144
chocolate industry 148–151
cholera 56, 58, 60, 61
class system 8, 66–67
climbing boys 136, 137
clothiers 14, 15
coal industry 26–27, 38, 51
coalfaces 27
coke 29
colonies 112, 114, 122
commuting 39
computers 43
constables 68
constipation 58
contaminate/contamination 58
costermongers 158
crime and punishment 68–69

D

dame schools 140
Darwin, Charles 73, 160–161
Declaration of the Rights of Man 98
dehydrate/dehydration 58
domestic system 14, 15
drawers 27
Ducking Stools 134
dysentery 83

E

education 66, 140–143
empires 92–97, 112–121
epidemics 58
Equiano, Olaudah 90
ether 144
evicted/eviction 163

F

factory reforms 30–31
factory system 17
factory towns 18–21
famine 162–165
Faraday, Michael 43
Fenians 164
Flying Shuttle 15
football 156–157
French Revolution 97–98

G

gallows 69
Great Exhibition 48–49
Great Hunger 162–165
Great Rebellion 121
Greenwich Mean Time (GMT) 38
guillotines 96

H

health and hygiene 12–13, 58–59, 144–147
high-streets 158–159
highwaymen 32
HMS Victory 104, 106–107
holidays 155
Home Rule 164

I

immigrants/immigration 12
impurities 46
independence 95, 164
India 114–121
indifferent personal qualities 84
Industrial Revolution 50–51
industry becomes mechanized 20
infantries 108, 109
inference 52
inferior/inferiority 134
invaders of India 116–117
invaders of North America 92–95
inventions (timeline) 46–47
Ireland 162–165
iron industry 28–29, 38, 51
ironworks 29

J

Jack the Ripper 74–77
Jenner, Edward 146

L

lashings/lashed (form of punishment) 86
leisure time 152–157
life expectancy 60, 65, 86
Lister, Joseph 146
literacy 13
living conditions 54–56, 60–61, 139
locomotives 36–37
logbooks 142
Louis XVI 96, 98
Lunar Society 20, 21

M

magistrates 68
manufacturing 50
marines 107
match girls 132–133
maternity care 12
mechanized industries 20
melodramas 152
Metropolitan Police 70
Middle Passage 79, 91
midwives 12
miners 26–27
modus operandi 76
music halls 152, 153
mutiny 118–121
muzzle (form of punishment) 86

N

Napoleon 99–101, 108–111
Native Americans 93
navvies 35
Nelson's touch 103–105
North America 92–95

O

okra 86
On the Origin of Species (Charles Darwin) 161
overseers 23, 25

P

Pasteur, Louis 146
pasteurization 146
pauper apprentices 22–25
Peterloo Massacre 127
philanthropists 138–139

phosphorus 132
plantations 86
police forces 70–71
population explosion 12–13
potato famine 162–165
power looms 17
prime ministers 9, 94, 162, 164
prison 72–73
protests 126–127
public health 60–65
punishment 68–69, 72–73

R

ragged schools 140
railways 38–39
raking 103
raw materials 51, 115
reforms/reformers 30–31, 129–131
Reign of Terror 98
revolt/revolution 87, 89, 126
roads 32–33
rotary motion 42

S

schools 66, 140–143
scrambles (for buying slaves) 84
seaside trips 155
Sepoys 118–121
sepsis 146
Seven Years War 95, 96
sewage 56, 64
sexist/sexism 135
Shaftesbury, Lord 137
sharpshooters 104, 107
shops 158–159
significance 20, 61
Six Acts 127
slave trade 78–91
slave trade triangle 78–79
smallpox 10, 12, 58, 83
snipers 107
Snow, John 62–63
social pyramids 66
spinning frames 16
Spinning Jenny 15
spinning mules 17
sport 154, 156–157
squalor 58
stagecoaches 32
steam engines 20, 42
Stephenson, George 36, 42
sterilize/sterilization 146
strikes 133
suburbs 39
'sun-and-planet' gear systems 20

T

TB (tuberculosis) 58
terraces 54
tolls/toll keepers 33
towns and their creation 18–21
transport systems 32–39
transportation (form of punishment) 69
trappers 27
tuberculosis (TB) 58
turnpike trusts 33
tutors 142
typhoid 58, 59

U

United States of America 96, 97

V

vaccinations 146
viaducts 36
viceroys 121, 123
Victoria, Queen 48, 120, 122, 126, 138, 144
voting 9, 128–131

W

War of Independence (America) 96–97
War of Independence (India) 118–121
watchmen 68
water frames 41
Watt, James 42
Waugh, Benjamin 138
Wedgwood, Josiah 34
Wellington, Duke of 108, 109, 126
women's rights 134–135
workhouses 139
wrought iron 28

Y

yams 86

OXFORD

UNIVERSITY PRESS

Great Clarendon Street, Oxford, OX2 6DP, United Kingdom

Oxford University Press is a department of the University of Oxford.
It furthers the University's objective of excellence in research,
scholarship, and education by publishing worldwide. Oxford is a
registered trade mark of Oxford University Press in the UK and in
certain other countries

British Library Cataloguing in Publication Data
Data available

978-0-19-839319-1

10 9

Paper used in the production of this book is a natural, recyclable
product made from wood grown in sustainable forests.
The manufacturing process conforms to the environmental
regulations of the country of origin.

Printed in Italy by L.E.G.O. S.p.A. Lavis (TN)

Acknowledgements

The publishers would like to thank the following for permissions to use their photographs:

p6: (t) Corbis/Christopher Cormack, (bl) © Bettmann/CORBIS, (br) Bridgeman Art Library; **p7**: (l) Georgios Kollidas/Shutterstock, (r) OUP; **p8**: Portrait of George III (1738-1820) in his Coronation Robes, c.1760 (oil on canvas), Ramsay, Allan (1713-84) / Private Collection / Bridgeman Images; **p9**: (t) Allan Staley/ Alamy, (b) The Village Fair, after 1710 (oil on copper), Michau, Theobald (1676-1765) / Private Collection / Johnny Van Haeften Ltd., London / Bridgeman Images; **p11**: Bettman/Corbis; **p15**: Getty Images/Hulton Archive; **p17**: Corbis/ Christopher Cormack; **p21**: The Heart of the West Riding, 1916 by Priestman, Bertram (1868-1951) © Bradford Art Galleries and Museums, West Yorkshire, UK/The Bridgeman Art Library; **p25**: Mary Evans Picture Library; **p30**: Mary Evans Picture Library; **p32**: Christie's Images Limited; **p34**: SSPL via Getty Images; **p36**: Mary Evans Picture Library; **p37**: (c) Michael Nicholson/Corbis; **p39**: (l, r) Thomas Cook Archives; **p40**: (tl) Georgios Kollidas/Shutterstock, (tml) E. T. Swift/Oxford University Press, (tmr) Art Directors.co.uk/Ark Religion. com, (tr) Helene Rogers/Art Directors and Trip Photo Library, (bl) Mary Evans Picture Library, (bml) Mary Evans/Epic/Tallandier, (bmr) © William Radcliffe/ Science Faction/Corbis, (br) © Steven Vidler/Corbis; **p41**: (t) Georgios Kollidas/ Shutterstock, (b) © DK Limited/CORBIS; **p42**: (t) E.T. Swift/Oxford University Press, (b) Art Directors.co.uk/Ark Religion.com; **p43**: (t) Helene Rogers/Art Directors and Trip Photo Library, (b) © Steven Vidler/Corbis; **p44**: (t, br) Mary Evans Picture Library, (bl) Mary Evans/Epic/Tallandier; **p45**: (l) © William Radcliffe/Science Faction/Corbis, (r) © Underwood & Underwood/Corbis; **p48**: Illustrated London News Ltd/Mary Evans; **p49**: Pictorial Press Ltd / Alamy; **p52**: Mary Evans Picture Library; **p54**: Mary Evans Picture Library; **p55**: (l) Getty Images/Mansell Collection/Time Life Pictures, (r) © North Wind Picture Archives/Alamy; **p58**: Mary Evans Picture Library; **p59**: The Water that John Drinks, © Punch Limited; **p60**: Mary Evans Picture Library; **p61**: Corbis/Hulton Archive; **p63**: The Wellcome Trust; **p64**: (t) Getty Images/Hulton Archive, (br) Mary Evans Picture Library, (l) Getty Images/Hulton Archive; **p69**: The Idle 'Prentice Executed at Tyburn, plate XI of 'Industry and Idleness', illustration from 'Hogarth Restored: The Whole Works of the celebrated William Hogarth, re-engraved by Thomas Cook', pub. 1812 (hand-coloured engraving), Hogarth, William (1697-1764)/Private Collection/The Stapleton Collection/The Bridgeman Art Library; **p71**: Mary Evans Picture Library; **p73**: Art Directors & Trip Photo Library; **p74**: Mirrorpix; **p75**: (t) Mary Evans Picture Library, (b) Mary Evans Picture Library/DAVID LEWIS HODGSON; **p78**: (t) © Stefano Bianchetti/Corbis, (b) Mary Evans/Everett Collection; **p80**: (t) Mary Evans/Everett Collection, (b) English Heritage Photo Library/The Bridgeman Art Library; **p81**: Tupungato/ Shutterstock; **p82**: (t) Mary Evans Picture Library, (b) Bridgeman Art Library; **p83**: Mary Evans/Everett Collection; **p84**: Mary Evans Picture Library; **p85**: (l, r) Bridgeman Art Library/Wilberforce House, Hull City Museums and Art Galleries, UK; **p86**: Bridgeman Art Library/British Library; **p87**: Western Reserve Historical Society Library, Cleveland, Ohio; **p88**: E. T. Swift/Oxford University Press; **p89**: Bettman/Corbis; **p90**: Bridgeman Art Library; **p91**: (tr) © STEPHEN HIRD/Reuters/Corbis, (bl) Bridgeman Art Library; **p95**: Mary Evans Picture Library/GROSVENOR PRINTS; **p96**: Execution of Louis XVI (1754-93) 21st January 1793 (coloured engraving), French School, (18th century)/Bibliotheque Nationale, Paris, France/Giraudon/The Bridgeman Art Library; **p97**: © FineArt / Alamy; **p98**: © Hulton-Deutsch Collection/CORBIS; **p99**: © Stefano Bianchetti/ CORBIS; **p101**: John Bull offering Little Boney fair play, published by Hannah Humphrey in 1803 (etching) by Gillray, James (1757-1815) © Courtesy of the Warden and Scholars of New College, Oxford/The Bridgeman Art Library; **p102**: Imagestate/HIP/The Print Collector; **p104**: Getty Images/Hulton Archive; **p105**: Corbis/John Harper; **p106**: © Skyscan/Corbis; **p108**: The Duke of Wellington (after Lawrence and Evans), 1834 (w/c on paper) by Derby, William (1786-1847) ©Wallace Collection, London, UK/The Bridgeman Art Library; **p109**: Paris - Musee de l'Armee, Dist. RMN/© Pascal Segrette; **p110**: The Turning Point at Waterloo (oil on canvas), by Hillingford, Robert Alexander (1825-1904); **p111**: The Battle of Waterloo, 18th June 1815 (oil on canvas) by Hillingford, Robert Alexander (1825-1904) Private Collection/The Bridgeman Art Library; **p114**: (l) Jayakumar/Shutterstock, (r) Casper1774 Studio/Shutterstock; **p115**: (t) holgs/ iStock, (m) © INTERFOTO/Alamy, (b) Ashwin82/iStock; **p116**: British Library/ HIP/TopFoto; **p117**: Mary Evans Picture Library; **p118**: The 7th Bengal Infantry on Parade, the Anglo-Indian Army of the 1880s (colour litho), Simkin, Richard (1840-1926) (after)/Private Collection/Peter Newark Pictures/Bridgeman Images; **p120**: © Bettmann/CORBIS; **p122**: (l) © Illustrated London News Ltd/Mary Evans, (r) raimond/iStock; **p123**: (l) © Hulton-Deutsch Collection/CORBIS, (r) Mary Evans Picture Library; **p126**: Royal Archives, Her Majesty Queen Elizabeth II; **p127**: Mary Evans Picture Library; **p128**: Bridgeman Art Library/Courtesy of the Trustees of Sir John Soane's Museum, London; **p130**: Punch Limited; **p132**: Mary Evans Picture Library; **p133**: (t) Mary Evans Picture Library, (b) © Illustrated London News Ltd/Mary Evans; **p134**: Harris Museum and Art Gallery, Preston, Lancashire, UK / The Bridgeman Art Library; **p135**: Richard Redgrave, R.A., The Outcast, 1851, Oil on canvas, 78.4 x 107.1 cm, ©Royal Academy of Arts, London, photographer: John Hammond; **p137**: (tl) Mary Evans Picture Library, (bl) © The Print Collector/ Alamy, (r) Kiev.Victor/Shutterstock; **p138**: (t) © Mary Evans Picture Library/Alamy, (b) Mary Evans Picture Library; **p139**: (t) With kind permission from Barnardo's, (b) © Hulton-Deutsch Collection/CORBIS; **p141**: Getty Images/Hulton Archive; **p142**: Mary Evans Picture Library; **p144**: Bridgeman Art Library/Royal College of Surgeons, London, UK; **p146**: Wellcome Trust Medial Photograph Library; **p147**: Wellcome Trust Medial Photograph Library; **p148**: (t) The Mariner's Museum, Newport News, VA, (b) Getty Images/Hulton Archive; **p149**: (t) Cadbury UK, (b) Mary Evans Picture Library; **p150**: (t, m, bl, br) Mary Evans Picture Library; **p153**: (t, b) Mary Evans Picture Library; **p154** (t) British Library/Robana via Getty Images; **p154-155**: Timelife Pictures/Mansell/Getty Images; **p156**: Mary Evans Picture Library; **p157**: (t, b) Mary Evans Picture Library; **p158**: Sotheby's Picture Library; **p159**: (l) Science & Society Picture Library, (r) Mary Evans Picture Library; **p160**: E.T. Swift/Oxford University Press; **p161**: (mc) Mary Evans Picture Library, (r) E.T. Swift/ Oxford University Press; **p163**: © Sean Sexton Collection/CORBIS; **p165**: © Alpha and Omega Collection/Alamy; **p169**: (l) Georgios Kollidas/Shutterstock, (ml) Mary Evans Picture Library, (m) Mary Evans Picture Library, (mr) Imagestate/HIP/The Print Collector, (r) Bridgeman Art Library

Artwork by Martin Sanders, Moreno Chiacchiera, QBS Media, Rudolf Farkas and Oxford University Press.

We are grateful for permission to reprint extracts from the following copyright texts.

J F Aylett: *In Search of History 1714-1900* (Hodder & Stoughton, 1985), copyright © J F Aylett 1985, and *The Suffragettes and After* (Hodder & Stoughton, 1987), copyright © J F Aylett 1987, reproduced by permission of Hodder Education.

Fédération Internationale de Football Association (FIFA): 'Football's Equipment Evolution', 26 April 2012, reproduced by permission of FIFA Communications.

Bob Fowke: *Who? What? When? Victorians* (Hodder Children's Books, 2003), reproduced by permission of the publishers.

Wes Magee: 'The Chimney Boy's Story (His Spirit Speaks)', copyright © Wes Magee 2000, from *The Phantom's Fang-Tastic Show* (OUP, 2000), reproduced by permission of the author.

James Morris: *Pax Brittanica* (Faber, 1968), copyright © James Morris 1968, reproduced by permission of United Agents (www.unitedagents.co.uk), on behalf of the author.

Bea Stimpson: *Quest: The World of Empire, Industry & Trade* (Stanley Thornes, 2000), reproduced by permission of Oxford University Press.

We have made every effort to trace and contact all copyright holders before publication, but if notified of any errors or omissions, the publisher will be happy to rectify these at the earliest opportunity.

From the author, Aaron Wilkes: Special thanks to Lois Durrant, my editor at OUP who has managed this project (and me) from beginning to end. Her energy, good humour and sound advice have been invaluable. Thanks also to the brilliant team at OUP who have helped deliver the various aspects of this package, in particular, Becky DeLozier, Janice Chan, Laura Syred and Fiona MacColl. In addition I am ever grateful to Sarah Flynn, my publisher, who continues to help develop, guide and support this series. I must also acknowledge my wife, Emma, and my daughters, Hannah and Eleanor, who continue to bring cups of tea and words of encouragement when I'm working late into the night.

The publishers would like to thank the following people for offering their contribution in the development of this book and related components: James Ball, for writing parts of the Second Editions of the books in this series. Patrick Taylor, Director of Teaching at Chenderit School, for literacy consultancy. Jerome Freeman, Educational Consultant, for assessment consultancy.

Links to third party websites are provided by Oxford in good faith and for information only. Oxford disclaims any responsibility for the materials contained in any third party website referenced in this work.